CRISIS
— IN —
CHRISTIAN
MUSIC

CRISIS
— IN —
CHRISTIAN
MUSIC

Volume II

The Paganization of Worship

by Dr. Jack Wheaton

Printed in the United States of America

ISBN 0-9744764-6-3

Contents

Introduction

The publication of my book *Crisis in Christian Music* by Hearthstone Publishing four years ago opened the door for honest debate regarding the rock invasion in the sanctuaries of our churches. In the meantime, others have stepped forward as well. At the time, I was being hired by various churches to help set up a "blended" religious service—one that combined traditional hymns and praise songs with some of the more musically and spiritually acceptable contemporary Christian music. Sadly, most blended services degenerated into rock hootenannies and all the good music was thrown out, along with parishioners who could no longer stomach the carnal atmosphere and the ear-splitting music.

The constant wars that I found going on in most churches over musical styles helped prompt me to write the first book. I was asked to be a guest on many of the leading Christian radio talk shows, including a series of four interviews with Southwest Radio Church. Mail began pouring in from all over the United States thanking me for writing the book and giving others objective guidelines for determining appropriate music for worship. Yes, there were some protest letters, but none of them could defend rock music in worship on a scriptural or honestly rational basis. Their primary argument: "It brings the young people in," and, "We like it!"

One argument was that the lyrics were spiritual even though the music was not. Unfortunately, in most instances, you could not clearly hear the lyrics and often when you could they were often childish, repetitious, and bordered on insult when singing to the Creator of the universe and His Son, Jesus Christ. Also, the sensual nature of much of the music always overpowers the lyric in situations like this.

Common sense told the church to keep worldly music out of the sanctuary. The church was successful in doing that for almost two thousand years.

What happened to change that? What happened was the most powerful musical style in history—rock music—emerged, using loud, sharp sounds to produce a drug-like effect on the human body (the fight-or-flight response) that was and is often mistaken in some modern churches for an outbreak of the Holy Spirit.

Another popular argument for Christian rock music in worship claimed that the only way to attract teenagers to church in today's society was to play the kind of music they liked. Wait a minute! I thought the Holy Spirit wooed the non-believer, and the prayers of friends and relatives helped. Are we supposed to be doing the work of the Holy Spirit using the most carnal music ever devised? I don't think so! You'll find some solid research in this new book that shoots holes in the theory that the kids won't come to church if they can't hear "their" music.

Finally, it's time for all of us who claim to know Jesus Christ to wake up and decide which end-time church we wish to be part of: the solid, biblically sound Philadelphian church, or the worldly but rich Laodicean church (both are described in Revelation 3). It's an important choice, because Scripture promises that the Philadelphian church *will not* "go through the time of trial that will come on the whole world" (the Tribulation), whereas the Laodicean church is promised a trip to the woodshed for their worldly ways.

The Jesus Movement that came out of the hippie culture of the 1960s and '70s brought a lot of zoned-out druggies into the kingdom. Sadly, we allowed them to bring two things into the sanctuary that had never been allowed before: loud, carnal "rock" music, now with "spiritual" lyrics, and slovenly dress. And so the compromise began. Thongs and bongos, electric guitars, men with long hair, and drums . . . lots of drums!

Not only did this new music invade our sanctuaries, but the old, traditional hymns (many that had been around for hundreds of years and sanctified in both lyrics and music) were tossed on the trash heap, no longer needed. The unbelievable arrogance and ego that allowed that to happen is enough to question the validity of these new sounds.

Common sense tells us that if the music is too loud, too repetitious, too sensual, too silly, or non-scriptural (lyrics), it is not appropriate for Christian worship. Common sense tells us that the deification of the major Christian rock stars is contrary to our role model, Jesus Christ, who reminded us to remain humble and to seek out the role of a humble servant. Common sense warns us that to use worldly means to achieve spiritual ends is a fatal compromise and leaves the door wide open to spiritual deception.

We ignored our spiritual intuition and common sense. We ignored our responsibility to guard the sanctuary from carnal entertainment and sensual music. We failed, and we will pay a price for it.

I have included both a biography and my testimony in this second book on Christian music. The reader should know my background so they can more legitimately evaluate my statements. I have spent a lot of time on radio and television interviews explaining my background, which I believe gives solid credibility to what is said in these pages.

Preface

This second volume of *Crisis in Christian Music* is designed to introduce more scientific evidence on the power of music on the human body, the brain, the emotions, and society. Music is a language of emotion that is impossible to censor. It is the most powerful and dangerous of all the art forms. Music can inspire, it can heal, it can hurt, and it can call up demonic forces that are contrary to everything our faith is based upon.

I've long held to the theory that, like cigarette smoking, we are just beginning to realize the potential dangers of certain styles of music. It's bad enough to see these new and dangerous musical styles creeping into our society. Its even worse to hear them introduced in our church as "sanctified" sounds when they are not.

I would like to thank my wife Jeanne for urging me to write this book, and Dr. Noah Hutchings of Southwest Radio Church for also encouraging me to add more solid information to the war of the musical styles in worship today.

It might be of interest to some of you to know that Christian rock music is a multibillion dollar a year industry. Sadly, Bible bookstores make more money from Christian rock records than they do from Bibles. It is worldly, it is powerful, and there are books out there that champion these sounds as being legitimate spiritually.

They are wrong. This includes Rick Warren, author of *The Purpose Driven Life*, who has attacked traditional hymns as being "elitist" and openly boasts of the ear-splitting volume of his music groups in his huge Mission Viejo, California, church.

In the world, the end may justify the means, but in the spiritual arena the means is just as important as the end. Trying to save sinners from the fires of Hell by playing music in church that came from the pit of Hell is an oxymoron; it will not work.

Christ warned us, "by their fruits ye shall know them." Examining the personal lives of many of the top Christian rock stars should tell us that there's something wrong, when the messenger is living a lifestyle contrary to the message.

The Tale of Two Churches

The Bible clearly indicates that in the "last days" there would be a major split in Protestant denominations. One would be "trendy," "seeker-sensitive," downplaying the fundamental doctrines of the faith (or ignoring them altogether), watering down the sinfulness of man and an ultimate destination for every human being: Heaven or Hell.

The Philadelphian Church

Christ gives us a quick review of church history in His analysis of the seven church types in Revelation 2–3. The final two churches are as different as night and day. Regarding the Philadelphian church, Christ had this to say:

> I know thy works: behold, I have set before thee an open door, and no man can shut it: for thou hast a little strength, and hast kept my word, and hast not denied my name. Behold, I will make them of the synagogue of Satan, which say they are Jews, and are not, but do lie; behold, I will make them to come and worship before thy feet, and to know that I have loved thee. Because thou hast kept the word of my patience, I also will keep thee from the hour of temptation, which shall come upon all the world, to try them that dwell upon the earth. Behold, I come quickly: hold that fast which thou hast, that no man take thy crown.
>
> —Revelation 3:8–11

A lengthy treatise or book could be written on this incredible passage alone. I will try to be concise in my evaluation of this passage and why it is so relevant to the subject of this book.

1. The Philadelphian type of church is operated by scriptural guidelines and reliance on the Holy Spirit for guidance, much as the early church did.

2. This church supports Israel, and believes Israel's rebirth in 1948 was an incredibly important fulfillment of prophecy. This church did not buy into the heretical teachings of Origen and Saint Augustine, who claimed that after the resurrection, all future prophecies concerning the Jews now belong to the church because the Jews forfeited the rights to these promises with their willingness to crucify Christ. *Nothing could be further from the truth.* Christ refers to this type of believer as belonging to the "synagogue of Satan" (pretty strong words). Christ goes on to say that some day this version of the Christian church will confess their error to the Philadelphian church.

3. The "open door" is the worldwide evangelist movement which began in England in the eighteenth century and continues today, largely through the efforts of the United States.

4. This church honors Christ as "God" and will not corrupt scripture or worship for worldly gain or success. This church is well aware of the wiles of Satan and his constant attacks on believers and his desire to pollute the sanctuary and the offering.

5. This church's worldly strength is limited. They are not rich and powerful like the Laodicean church, nor do they covet riches or power.

6. Because this church has resisted attempts at ecumenicalism (the bringing together of "all" types of faiths under one banner, fads and trends in worship, the introduction of worldly music, non-biblical counseling, etc.), *they are promised to be spared from the final seven years before Christ comes back, the Tribulation, that horrible period in human history described so graphically in Revelation 6–19.* This promise confirms the mystery of the Rapture, that startling worldwide event described so vividly in Scripture.

7. Christ offers additional promises to this church, the one that remained loyal to the Word of God and the guidance of the Holy Spirit. He promises that they will be made "pillars" in His temple (essential and important). He will write on them His new name, and they will have free access to the New Jerusalem, when it appears.

This church will remain humble, Christ-centered, biblically literate, highly suspicious of the world and its allures and aware of Satan's wiles. It will resist the temptation to "reach" more potential believers through doctrinal compromise and worldly entertainment. This church understands that being faithful, hopeful, obedient, and humble are its primary tasks. *No rock music in this church!*

Laodicean Church

Christ describes this church in the following manner:

> I know thy works, that thou art neither cold nor hot: I would thou wert cold or hot. So then because thou art lukewarm, and neither cold nor hot, I will spue thee out of my mouth. Because thou sayest, I am rich, and increased with goods, and have need of nothing; and knowest not that thou art wretched, and miserable, and poor, and blind, and naked: I counsel thee to buy of me gold tried in the fire, that thou mayest be rich; and white raiment, that thou mayest be clothed, and that the shame of thy nakedness do not appear; and anoint thine eyes with eyesalve, that thou mayest see. As many as I love, I rebuke and chasten: be zealous therefore, and repent.
>
> —Revelation 3:15–19

Christ goes on to tell this church that He's *outside* the church, knocking to get back in. When the sanctuary of the church is polluted with demonically-inspired music, or worldly, carnal entertainment and "charismatic" personality-types in the pulpit *the Holy Spirit is grieved and flees.*

In every worship service either Satan and his demonic hordes are driven away through sanctified music, the reading of the Word, confession of sin, and the lifting up of the name of Jesus Christ, or Christ and the Holy Spirit are driven away by the paganization, rebellion, idolatry, and pride of the church presenting polluted worship and sacrifice. *There is no middle ground.* When you give into worldly power to gain members you lose spiritual power.

False Spiritual Power

Before I came to know the Lord, I was lusting for spiritual power. I got it. I used creative visualization, meditation, chanting, and other rituals to trigger an outpouring of worldly goods and success. I thought all this was coming from God. It wasn't. It was coming from Satan. He was bribing me with the world's goodies to try to pacify me in my hunger to find the one true God. I became increasingly filled with pride and disdainful of others.

Remember, Satan is still "prince of this world." He can hand out temporal rewards for faithfulness to his dark side. In the occult world—Satan's world—spiritual power comes through an increasing self-centeredness and an unawareness that your worship is being directed to him via the intermediary of a mantra, a guru, a false religious leader or book, an object, special music, chanting, etc. There is an invisible chain on the end of Satan's bribes. He can take them away at any moment and our loyalty to him, even though we may not be aware of it because it occurs through an intermediary, is rewarded by an eternity in Hell, separated forever from all that is good, beautiful, loving, forgiving, kind, and joyous.

True Spiritual Power

The irony of biblical, scriptural, true Christianity is that true spiritual power is only available to the degree that we die to self and place Christ and others before ourselves. If pride is the driving force behind all satanic power, humility is the driving force behind all true spiritual power. Joy is defined in believing in Christ in the following manner:

Jesus first + others second + yourself last = Joy!

The apostle Paul said in one of his epistles; "I die daily." Each of us must die to self daily to grow in Christ. Music either helps or hinders our desires in this area, depending on the sanctification of the music.

Rock Music

Rock music is built on a foundation of pride, rebellion, sensuality, and paganism. It has no place in true worship, regardless of the words of the songs. I have interviewed, performed with, and written arrangements and compositions for many major "Christian" artists. Most are as egotistical, prideful, and self-centered as any artists I have worked with in the secular world. In some instances, many popular Christian rock stars are worse, because they hide behind a false religious system, and lure many innocent young people into a wayward faith and worship that is not acceptable to God.

I would not want to be in their shoes when they stand before a righteous God and explain their motivation for being disobedient, sensual, and worldly. I personally have asked forgiveness for misleading any believers through the music I've performed, composed, arranged, or recorded. I am finishing an Easter cantata as I write this, and I'm asking the Lord to guide me so that it is humbly presented, scripturally sound, and acceptable worship.

Two Churches

The dramatic fulfillment of end-time prophecy is here today in so many ways. Certainly the prophecy of two different branches of the Christian church is being fulfilled before our very eyes. The characteristics of both are outlined in Revelation 3, given to the apostle John on the isle of Patmos almost two thousand years ago.

The most sobering gift God gave each of us is free will. To not have free will would be to be as robots. God could never be sure of our love unless we have the *option* of choosing not to love Him. Each of you must choose. Spiritual deception is rampant. To remain true in our faith we all must spend more time in prayer and in Bible study. We must be more sensitive to the indwelling of the Holy Spirit, who will guide us if we learn to listen to that still small voice and confess our sins daily (1 John 1:9) so that there is not a barrier between us and God.

This is serious business. None of us wants to go through the final seven years before Christ's return. The Philadelphian church is promised to be spared this fate; the Laodicean church is promised discipline—until they repent.

The world does not belong in the church. However, the church does belong in the world, and even more so, now that the end of the age is approaching. Christ left two commandments for His followers: love one another and go out into the world and spread the "good news" (gospel) and/or support those that do.

Take a stand. If your church is determined to sell out to worldly ways, compromise your faith, pollute the sanctuary, and offer up unsuitable worship to a holy God, *get out of that church.* Do not support idolatrous, worldly ministries, no matter how outwardly attractive and powerful they are.

Humility is the most important virtue in a Christian's life. The second, in my opinion, is courage. Have the courage to defend the faith, always with love, but never compromising the basic doctrines of our faith nor the Word of God. Care less what man thinks of you and be more concerned with what God thinks of you. As a believer, you will spend eternity with God, not man. Concentrate on building up those spiritual treasures that last.

On a Personal Note

I have received some criticism for writing the first volume of *Crisis in Christian Music*. Fellow musicians who are involved in carnal music for the worldly church are puzzled by my stand. Give up fame and fortune? Other publishers are wary of my books. Bible bookstores seldom mention or carry my books because the truths I expose could effect their income.

Certainly I am no longer available to write arrangements and/or songs for those worldly Christian artists. I have been a guest on many Christian talk shows, but seldom does a pastor or a church or even Christian musical organizations ask me to speak. *They are afraid of conviction.*

Christian rock music is now a $3 *billion* a year industry. Bookstores make most of their money from recorded Christian rock CDs. Superstars make millions, and televangelists who support this kind of carnal music and present a watered-down message have annual incomes in the $25–50 million range. *They have sold their souls for worldly power, money, and fame.*

However, no one can seriously question my credentials in writing these books, nor can they question my intent. They can only argue against the case I have made for tightening up the qualifications for sanctified music and performers. Their arguments are always based on worldly principles: pride, profit, and growth. They have no scriptural foundation and they know it.

I pray for all the churches, pastors, elders, deacons, musicians, congregations, bookstores, publishers, and recording labels that have become rich, sleek, and powerful shoveling the devil's music into the mouths and ears of young Christians. I pray they will repent, that they will seek God's face and turn from their wicked ways. Their style of music is polluted, the sanctuary is polluted, worship has been paganized, and congregations have been misled. It's time to sweep out the temple and turn over the tables of the money changers once again. Christ is our role model. If He had the courage to do it, not once but twice, then what are we waiting for?

Music Is . . .

Some types of music can lift our soul, and awaken the spirit of prayer, compassion, and love. Some styles of music clear our minds and make us smarter. Different styles of music can sing our blues away, or bring back memories of old friends. Music lets the child in us play, the religious pray, the cowboy to line dance, the physically and emotionally ill to heal.

Wide Varieties in Style

Music can be holy or profane. Music can build or it can tear down. Music can heal the mind or tear the mind apart. Music can heal the body or it can destroy internal organs and negatively affect our immune system and our automatic nervous system. Music can bring relaxation or it can push us to the point of a nervous breakdown. Music can cure the blues and stop suicide—or the reverse

There has never been a major religious, political, or social movement without music to lead it. Every nation has its national anthem; every married couple has "their song." Music leads a man into battle, and gives hope to those back home.

Music can bring Jesus and His angels, or music can conjure up Satan and his demons. Music is the bridge to Heaven or the bridge to Hell. Music is so powerful that around 400 B.C. the ancient Greek philosopher Plato said, "I do not care what subjects you teach in your schools and universities. Let me teach and control music and I will control your society."

What the Experts Say

Research has found that *shrill sounds of sufficient volume* can congeal proteins in a liquid media. A soft egg placed in front of a speaker at a loud rock concert can midway through the concert become *a hard-boiled snack for the weary headbanger* (Bob Larson, *The Day the Music Died*, Bob Larson Ministries, 1974).

Plants respond positively to classical forms of music, actually growing and flowering faster than if there *was no music at all*. Conversely, more dissident forms of music, like heavy metal (rock), can *actually retard growth and even kill the plant* (Tame, *The Secret Power of Music*, p. 143).

Musicologist Dr. Adam Knieste said: "Music is really a *powerful drug*. Music can poison you, lift your spirits, or make you sick without knowing why" (David Chagall, *Family Weekly Magazine*, January 30, 1983, p. 12).

There is mounting evidence that certain kinds of rock music have a negative effect on one's ability to think and learn. Studies at two separate universities, for example, have found that rats have a much more difficult time learning to pass through a maze *if they are subjected to hard rock music* (*Insight*, April 27, 1987, p. 57).

Music has an inside track to the subconscious levels of our minds. This truth is even physically suggested by the fact that the auditory nerves are *the most predominant of all the human senses* (Tame, pp. 136, 148–150).

Research at Stanford University confirms that in the area of transcendent experiences (what the researchers term *thrills*) they found that the most powerful stimulus for evoking thrill-like sensations in their subjects *was music*. (Abram and Goldstein, *Physiological Psychology*, 1980, vol. 8 [1] pp. 126–129).

Spiritual Dimension

Music was Satan's responsibility. Before his fall he was in charge of worship and music (Isa. 14; Ezek. 28). Satan and his army of occult experts (demons) can pervert any form of music. However, rock music is today the most dangerous tool Satan has in his arsenal because of its unparalleled popularity, its subtle and generally unknown factor that it can be used as a drug, and the swift descent into evil by its practitioners.

In 2 Corinthians, the apostle Paul warns us that Satan's favorite disguise is as *an angel of light*. Satan wants to compromise and corrupt the pure worship of our Lord and Savior Jesus Christ, because a growing, knowledgeable body of Christ can *clip his wings* faster than any other method. Satan fears (and respects) holiness, the Word of God, and sincere and sanctified prayer.

He will do everything he can to corrupt or co-opt the Body of Christ, because he's running out of time.

> I do believe that music itself is a spiritual force. The inspiration I feel is like a holy thing. It's beyond any words I can use to describe it.
>
> —Avant-garde musician Peter Rowan, *Washington Times*, March 7, 1986

> One night we were playing and suddenly the spirit entered into me and I was playing but it was no longer me playing.
>
> —John McGlaughlin, well-known rock guitarist-composer, *Circus*, April 1972, p. 38

> Someone else is steering me. I'm just along for the ride. I become possessed when I'm on stage.
>
> —AC/DC guitarist Angus Young, *Hit Parade*, 1985

Be Sober, Be Vigilant

Are we too naïve? Why do we not understand that one of Satan's greatest thrills is to pervert or contaminate sacrifice and worship offered up to a holy God. A sanctified worship service is a tremendous threat to him and his evil demons. Satan does everything he can to keep sinners from coming to Christ. His next priority is to oppress believers and lead them into carnal paths. His third priority is to contaminate worship so that the prayers are not received in Heaven.

We need to awaken and be aware of his agenda and learn how to resist him in these areas. I pray that this book will help in this task.

The Seven Ingredients in Music

What Is Music?

What is music? Isn't it interesting that something we take for granted like music we actually know very little about? We know music is sound. In fact, a simple definition of music would be *organized sound*. The opposite of music would be noise—obviously, disorganized sound.

One thing to keep in mind: music is a language of emotion. The auditory nerves are part of the mid-brain (hypothalamus) that is also the seat of our emotions. You cannot censor your reaction to music, because your emotions are triggered before your cerebral cortex (seat of intellect) can control them. That is one of the reasons music is so powerful.

We know music to be powerful. There has never been a major religious or social movement without music. Every nation has its national anthem. Children grow up singing nursery rhymes. Major holidays and important historical events are celebrated in song. Man cannot worship without music. Man cannot express love without music.

Music can inspire, it can heal, it can destroy, it can calm, it can excite, it can prepare you for love, war, worship, maternity. In some tribal cultures the entire history of the tribe is transcribed, stored, and narrated to future generations through music. So what is music made of?

Parts

Music can be broken into seven categories of sound. Not all music has all seven categories, but to comprehensively define music we must include all seven. They are (in order of importance) rhythm, form, melody, countermelody, harmony, textures (tone, range, voicing), and style (tempo—fast or slow, dynamics—loud or soft, and articulation—short or long notes). Defining musical styles is just a matter of defining the favorite clichés used in each of these categories.

Clichés

Each of these parts of music has standard musical clichés for personal and historical styles. One can quickly define and imitate any musical style by breaking the example in parts and then analyzing the parts for historical and personal styles. For instance, Mozart had favorite clichés that he used often in his writing. By studying these clichés, one can write music in the style of Mozart. There are computer programs today that are actually composing music using this system.

So, let's now examine the seven parts of a musical composition, starting with the most important—rhythm.

Rhythm

Rhythm is the oldest part of music, the part that we are most sensitive to, and the part of music that is the most powerful. I believe that rhythm is so important because the human body is rhythmic. As I write this, my circulatory system, respiratory system, endocrine system, digestive system, and other parts of my body move in rhythmic patterns. Muscles contract and relax when walking, running, or dancing. Our speech is rhythmic as well. (For more information on the subject of rhythm, see the chapter devoted to this most important element of music).

Rhythm and the Body

The rhythms of music can affect the rhythm patterns of our body. For instance, the military traditionally played marches in the morning for the troops. Why? Because it helped them wake up faster. The respiratory rate slows down during sleep to 70 counts per minute or slower. The average march is around 124 counts per minute. *The body tries to adapt to the steady rhythms of the march.* Today we do it with Jazzercise. For centuries in both primitive and civil societies men went to war to the sound of drums. Today it's rock music—but still the sound of drums.

Melody

Some anthropologists suggest that singing preceded speech. Many of the world's languages are phonetic—in the sense that a word can mean several different things, depending on the pitch of the voice. This is particularly true in tribal African languages and many of the Asian dialects. Some of the things we have learned about melody:

1. Ascending melodies create tension; descending melodies release tension.
2. There are four categories of intervals: perfect, consonant, mild–dissonant, and dissonant. Each type of interval suggests a particular type of emotion.
3. Melodies are built on scales and modes. Different ethnic and cultural groups use different scales. For instance Asians favor the pentatonic (five-tone) scale, while Arabic cultures favor what we call the "Middle Eastern scale." Then we have the very popular "blues" scale—so common to Afro-American music in the United States.
4. Repetitive melodies can induce a low level of self-hypnosis.
5. Most popular melodies build slowly to a climax note (usually the highest note) at least two-thirds of the way through the tune.
6. Long-term memory is in the right brain hemisphere. Musical skills are predominately right-brain. One of the reasons music is used so often to sell a product on radio or television is because we will remember the product because of the melody.

Counter-melody

The next development in music was the introduction of a second voice that contrasts with the first voice. In ancient plainsong in the Catholic Church in Europe, the introduction of a contrapuntal or second-voice melody combining with another melody was a major breakthrough in the development of music in Western Europe.

Today, a melody with an accompanying bass-line is contrapuntal. The height of contrapuntal writing skill was found in the Baroque music (1685–1750) of Johann Sebastian Bach.

Harmony

Harmony is the combining of two or more notes with a melody note simultaneously. The sounding of three notes together is a "chord." A three-note chord is also called a "triad." Once notes were organized into chords we begin to have chord progressions. *The invention of the keyboard drove the harmonic system.* Again, one of the important parts of music that separates Western European musical tradition and that of most of the rest of the world is the highly developed system of harmony. *Most tribal music of the world does not have a harmonic system.* When harmony is used in tribal African music for instance, it is randomly introduced.

Texture

Texture includes three important parts: pitch (high or low), tone (bright, clear, dark, raspy), and chord voicings (closed or open). All three have a dramatic effect on the message of the music. High voicings suggest delicacy, vulnerability; low pitch suggests power, danger, darkness; mid-range suggests comfort and security, because it parallels our vocal range.

Bright texture is exciting, glittering; clear texture suggests purity, innocence; dark suggests rich, sexy; and raspy—a favorite African texture—suggests energy, tension. The human voice is capable of expressing all four textures, and there are many instruments that express two or more different textural tones.

When all the notes in the chord are as close together as possible the chords are said to be in "closed" position. When the notes are spread over a wide acoustical range the chords are said to be in "open" position. Then there is a partially open voicing, as well. Closed voicing suggests forward movement, energy. Open voicing suggest power.

Style

Like the above, the category of "style" is made up of three parts: tempo, dynamics, and articulation. Tempos reflect moods. Moods of love, repose, and inspiration are seldom fast. Moods of anger, excitement, and anticipation are seldom slow.

Dynamics likewise reflect moods. Soft sounds are introspective, romantic, and soothing. Loud sounds suggest danger, rage, excitement, and power. Loud sounds can also trigger the fight-or-flight response that causes the body to go into a crisis mode and stimulates hard-to-control moods of aggression, anxiety, and anger.

Articulation describes whether or not the notes flow smoothly one to another without interruption, or the opposite, the notes are short with as much space between them as possible. Connected notes are called "legato." Separated notes are called "staccato." Legato notes are soothing, sensual, and relaxing. Staccato notes suggest tension, discipline, and anger.

Summary

As a film composer I had to learn to quickly analyze various musical styles and decide which combinations were the most appropriate for the drama taking place on the screen. I also had to learn to write in a wide range of historical, cultural, and pop styles. Finally, I tried to match the musical clichés used to the most predominant emotions being displayed on the screen at the time. Interestingly enough, there are seven basic human emotions: mad, sad, glad, scared, sensual, humorous, and inspirational.

When the music matches the emotion you have succeeded.

I have found that learning this skill of analysis has not only enhanced my writing and improvisational skills, it has also enhanced my enjoyment and appreciation of the great composers and their phenomenal skills in manipulating our emotions through the power of music.

What's Wrong with Christian Rock Music?

Volume. It's too loud. The volume is not only potentially damaging to the hearing of the musicians and the congregation, but it triggers the "fight or flight" response and additional adrenaline is pumped into the blood stream, making us feel aggressive and sometimes angry. Is this the mood we wish to create for worship?

Lyrics. The words are usually inane, sophomoric, and separated from solid scriptural concepts. Compare even one line of a standard great hymn like *A Mighty Fortress Is Our God* with *Our God Is an Awesome God* and you will see what I mean.

Repetitive. When Christ warned His followers in Matthew 6 not to "babble" like the heathen when praying or worshipping, He was referring to a common practice of cultic religions of the times. *Constant repetition of simplistic lyrics creates a hypnotic state that allows unseen forces to mess with your mind.*

Breaks with Tradition. For almost two thousand years the church, both Catholic and Protestant, separated music into sacred and secular. Secular music was for the world; sacred music was for the church. *Christian rock is an attempt to smuggle secular music into worship.* I love to play jazz. However, I would *never* advocate jazz in a worship service. Jazz music was and is *secular; it does not belong in worship. Neither does so-called "Christian" rock.*

Market Driven. The music is market-driven. It has a commercial agenda. Today Christian rock is one of the fastest growing parts of the secular recording industry. Its annual gross is approaching $3 billion. Most Christian bookstores survive today not on the sales of their Bibles, but of their CDs, DVDs, and Christian novels.

Ignores Tradition. Not only has Christian rock stuck their foot in the door, they have had the arrogance to throw out most traditional Christian music. On what basis? Are you telling me that the hymns of Fannie Crosby, Martin Luther, the Wesleys, and others, are no longer appropriate for worship? *On what basis? What criteria?*

The eagerness and arrogance on the part of the practitioners of Christian rock to dispose of the past disqualifies them for worship. I thought *humility* was the most important virtue taught in Scripture. I see no humility here.

Dangerous Rhythms. I spent ten years researching the material for my book *All That Jazz: A History of Afro-American Music*, and I discovered something very disturbing. Most of the ancient tribal religions of Africa, Asia, India, Indonesia, and Polynesia used certain rhythms in their worship rituals to *attract demons*. These "forces" from another world were the centerpiece of their worship. Today many of these same rhythms have crept into the mainstream of American music through jazz, blues, rock, and now Christian rock. *They are spiritually dangerous and certainly do not belong in a Christian worship service.*

Christian "Divas" and "Artists." Big names in Christian rock arrive in limousines, live in million-dollar mansions, and travel with a retinue of followers that immolates movie stars and rock stars. There is no difference—except in the lyrics of the songs they sing, and increasingly, major Christian rock artists are singing secular rock tunes without an apology in their concerts and on their CDs.

Role of Music in Worship Misunderstood. In the early church (A.D. 32–350), music was used at the beginning of the service to (1) unify the body of believers, (2) introduce the theme of the sermon or scripture reading, (3) drive away demonic forces by lifting the name of Jesus in song, and (4) inspire humility, devotion, confession, and service. *Music never was and never should have been used to entertain, dazzle, or distract as it to often used today.*

Poor Craftsmanship. So much contemporary Christian music is childish in concept. Melodies are sometimes nonexistent, sing-song, or more often on the level of a child's nursery rhyme. Where are the great, soaring melodies like *How Great Thou Art, The Church's One Foundation*, and many others? The rhythm patterns are usually simplistic or unnecessarily complicated and repetitive.

Boring. Lyrics, as we've already mentioned, are seldom solid scripturally, and the repetitiveness sets up a hypnotic situation that is dangerous. Arrangements are usually for garage-band instrumentation: one or two electric guitars, electric bass, sometimes a keyboard, and drums. The variation in sounds available to this type of group compared to an orchestra or even the organ is laughable. Same sounds, same type of songs and lyrics . . . boring, boring, boring!

Musicianship. Many contemporary Christian rock musicians are poorly trained. Many of them, like their millionaire commercial rock counterparts, cannot read music. Their limited exposure to traditional Christian music gives them little to build their talent on. Sadly, most of these musicians are not good enough to make it in the commercial rock world, so they flip over into rock church music, hoping not only to get a "gig" at a local church, but to work up the food chain through CDs and concerts until they too have their own customized tour bus and a large bank account.

Common Sense. Common sense should tell us, as it has through history until this point, that the church should be a "sanctuary" from the trials, tribulations, and evils of the world. Most people, when they go to church, want to get away from the world, not greet it again. *Surprisingly, surveys show that this is just as true for teenagers.* People are looking for something solid, something that's been around awhile, and something that is not subject to the commercial pressures of the market place. People want church to be quiet, dignified, uplifting, worshipful, and holy. Holiness is important—it reminds us of our eternal nature, which is wrapped in this temporary body.

Common sense tells us that Christian rock is an oxymoron and does not belong in the sanctuary, in worship, and in lifting up the name of our Lord and Savior, Jesus Christ. Notice I said *Christian rock*. There is plenty of room for the truly spiritually inspired in Christian music today, like the Brooklyn Tabernacle Choir, Andre Crouch, Bill Gaither, and others.

David Wilkerson. David Wilkerson, author of *The Cross and the Switchblade,* was a pastor in a small Midwestern town for years. He decided to begin tithing his time as well as his talent and money. As he moved deeper into extended periods of prayer, he felt the Lord calling him to New York City to minister to the gangs, drug dealers, and prostitutes.

He has written several books since *The Cross and the Switchblade.* One of his most powerful, a warning to lukewarm Christians in the United States, is his book *Set the Trumpet to Thy Mouth* (Whitaker House, 1985). David has a very serious chapter in this book dealing with Christian rock music in the church. He emphasizes four reasons why this style of music does not belong in worship service:

1. *Out of which womb was the music born?* Can we like alchemists, turn satanically–inspired secular music into sacred music, acceptable to God by changing a few words here and there? The author says "no" and gives multiple scriptural references to support his points (Isa. 6:43, 48:8; Ps. 22:9–10, 58:3–5; Hos. 9:9–12; Mark 12:17; Matt. 7:18–19; Luke 1:15; Jer. 7,10–11).

2. *God will not accept a blemished sacrifice.* Throughout the Old Testament, carnal believers thought they could fool God by sacrificing blemished animals. *Never did it fool God for a minute.* In the New Testament, Christ drove the moneychangers out of the Jewish temple in Jerusalem *twice:* once at the beginning of His ministry and then just before His crucifixion. I cringe when I see tables set up in the lobbies of churches today pushing CDs, T-shirts, posters, etc., of some so-called "Christian rock" star "performing" that day for worship. What would Christ do if He saw and heard all this? On page 130 of *Set the Trumpet to Thy Mouth,* David Wilkerson says: "God Himself called His church a *house of sacrifice* (2 Chron. 7:12). *Every time a child of God preaches, prays, praises, or sings, he is bringing a sacrificial offering unto the Lord. Every Christian concert or recording is an offering unto the Lord* (Exod. 12:5; Eph 4:29; Mal. 1:8,13,24.)"

3. Changing the lyrics does not change the intent: "I hear sincere Christians say, 'Satan doesn't own music. It belongs to God. The music doesn't matter as long as the words are right.' Dead wrong? *The Devil owns all music that is ungodly and evil.* Satan had all the *right words* when he tempted Christ (he even quoted scripture, part of Psalm 91). The Israelites dancing around the golden calf (in Exodus) had all the right words. Were they not singing, *'This is the god that brought us out of Egypt?'* Same people, same music, same words—*but their God had changed.* Satan has *always* spoken in temptation with accurate words mingled with a lot of Scrip-

ture, and so has every angel of light who has come to deceive. (That's why Christ compared sin to 'leaven'—it is always 'hidden' and it always 'puffs up.') I've noticed that musicians at Christian concerts seldom perform rock just before the message and invitation. *It is not conducive to conviction of any kind because it is of another spirit*" (David Wilkerson, *Set the Trumpet to Thy Mouth*, p. 132).

4. God has His prescribed boundaries for worship (Mal. 1:7,12; Prov. 13:14; 2 Kings 2:23 [the mocking of holiness]; Ps. 141:5; Isa. 66:4, 48:8). "There is an attitude among rock fans who are Christian that truly frightens me. They become *sold out to it; they promote it with zeal; they will not give it up, not even for Jesus and the Holy Spirit it is so deeply embedded in their hearts*" (Wilkerson, *Trumpet*, p. 134).

Meekness vs. Timidity. Meekness does not mean timidity. Christ's example of driving the money changers from the temple, and His scathing indictment in John 8 of the religions leaders of the time, are examples of the importance of standing up to evil, *particularly when it tries to enter the sanctuary and pollute worship.* If you are in a church that has rock music as the focal point of its worship, *get out!* Warn the pastor, the music director, and the worship director; give them copies of my books and/or many of the other books mentioned in this treatise or in the bibliography. *But have the courage to take a stand.* Remember, each of us who have accepted Jesus Christ as our Lord and Savior will stand before Him someday, not for judgment but for reward; He will ask us, *Do you love Me, and what have you done for me?*

> **For other foundation can no man lay than that is laid, which is Jesus Christ.** Now if any man build upon this foundation gold, silver, precious stones, wood, hay, stubble; Every man's work shall be made manifest: for the day shall declare it, because it shall be revealed by fire; and the fire shall try every man's work of what sort it is. If any man's work abide which he hath built thereupon, he shall receive a reward. If any man's work shall be burned, he shall suffer loss: but he himself shall be saved; yet so as by fire.
> —1 Corinthians 3:11–15

Spiritual Deception. We live in those times the Bible calls the "end times."

Christ warned us in the Olivet Discourse (Matt. 24–25; Mark 13; Luke 21) that the primary characteristic of this final age would be *spiritual deception*. As a believer in Jesus Christ, the infallibility of the Bible, the indwelling of the Holy Spirit—as a musician, historian, and writer—*Christian rock music does not belong in the sanctuary of any non-apostate church.*

To allow it in to attract more young people is a fallacious argument. It is making a deal with the devil, one that every truly born-again believer will live to regret, from the Christian rock "superstars," through the television evangelists, the local church, pastors, elders, deacons, and musicians. *God holds us responsible for our behavior,* but He forgives our sins when we identify them, confess them *and turn from them* (1 John 1:9).

As you read this book, keep in mind that as a musician I know how to write, play, and compose Christian rock music. I could enter this field and possibly make a large amount of money and even fool myself that I was doing the Lord's work. It would take a lot pride and lying to myself to go that route after what I know. I thank the Lord Jesus Christ every day for sending the Holy Spirit to rescue me in August 1973 from the pit of Hell, for forgiving my chronic relapses and rebelliousness over the years, for slowly (through prayer, fellowship, knowledge of Scripture, and a devoted, loving Christian wife) bringing me to a place I thought I would never reach, nor could I reach on my own. Many friends and relatives have not been as fortunate.

Secular as Well as Sacred. I am not only trying to warn the church of the danger of this style of music, but I am writing at the same time another book entitled *The Power of Music* (Scarecrow Press) that has a vast amount of recent scientific evidence that rock music is just as dangerous and deadly as illegal drugs and has weakened our society and impacted the health, educationability, and morals of several generations of those who grew up with this deadly dangerous art form called "rock."

If you read this book with an open, prayerful, humble mind, you cannot but agree that rock music is tainted, polluted, and dangerous. If you turn from the truths given here and in many other books, web sites, articles, sermons, etc., and continue to support this evil disguised as "good," then you are entering dangerous waters spiritually.

I prayerfully urge you, a fellow believer in Jesus Christ, to soberly consider the scriptures, facts, and opinions presented here. May the Lord bless

you and keep you if you do; and may He give you the courage to turn away
from the most powerful secular musical style ever to visit our planet, one that
has caused considerable harm to the unsaved as well and has infected the
saved with a salvation-weakening virus.

The only known antidote, like AIDS, is abstinence and total rejection of
its alluring charms.

The Paganization of Worship

Whereas many conservatives preached what amounts to "Clean yourself up before you receive Christ," the Jesus movement (where Contemporary Christian Music began) said more biblically, "Come as you are." The problem however was that come as you are more often meant "remain as you are," at least as far as music, language, clothing and social habits are concerned.

—John Makujina, *Measuring the Music*, page 208

The Pollution of the Sanctuary

Been to church lately? If not, you're in for a surprise! No more do you go to church to worship, find silence, escape from the world, turn within, seek inner healing. Church today, with few exceptions, has become more of a combination pep rally, rock concert, and sales expo. Jesus is your "buddy," you're His "friend," and everything is cool! Those over fifty years in age—adjust or stay home! Here are some of the typical changes that have taken place:

Environment

Probably the "church" will look more like a mall, a movie theater, or an auditorium. Pews are outdated; folding chairs or movie-theater type seating is "in." You will find no Bibles or hymnals, because everything important will be flashed on a large screen on each side of the platform of the sanctuary.

There will be no stained-glass windows, tapestries, paintings, or other reminders of the almost two thousand years of church history. There will be slogans—in large letters—across the front, and special lighting, once the music starts. You may or may not find a cross behind the pulpit because some new "seeker-sensitive" worshippers might be offended by it.

People will enter dressed as casually as they wish: thongs and cut-offs (shorts) are not unusual. What is unusual is anyone who "dresses" for church out of respect for God and tradition.

Rather than contemplative silence with soft organ or piano music before the service, social banter and loud talking are the norm. Those closing their eyes or bowing their heads in somber silence are looked on with suspicion by the "regulars."

A high percentage of the church bulletin reports on social activities of the church, with an often hard-to-find outline of the service thrown in. Scripture in the bulletin is usually brief, when found. It's important for the church to be busy-busy-busy with all kinds of activities. Yes, there are Bible studies, but they are not given preeminence in their billing. They are just another "take it or leave it" activity. You begin to feel that the church is more of a country club for those who "dig" Jesus than a place of worship and discipleship.

People are superficially friendly, but with a "take it or leave it" attitude if you begin asking pointed questions about the demise of traditional worship.

The word "sanctuary" is a joke. There is little difference between the environment just outside the worship service and that within. In other words, the world has invaded the sanctuary and driven a sense of "holiness" out. People talk and fidget and move around until the music cranks up, and I do mean crank up.

Music

Once you have decided on the style of music you're going to use in worship, you have set the direction of your church in far more ways than you realize. It will determine the kind of people you attract, the kind of people you keep, and the kind of people you lose.

—*The Purpose-Driven Church*, Rick Warren, page 280

Ah, the music. Looking for the organ? It's not there. Looking for a robed choir? They're gone! Looking for a piano? It may be there, but is used only for contrast to the rock musicians who are assembling on the platform with a small group of "singers" dressed as if they were headed for the beach.

This type of ensemble is called a "praise band." They have replaced choirs, church orchestras, organists, and pianists. Generally a praise band is made up of drums, electric bass, two electric guitars, synthesizer, and sometimes one or two wind instruments, usually trumpet and trombone or saxophone.

This is the same instrumentation you will find on stage at most rock concerts. A coincidence? I don't think so. So-called contemporary Christian music today is the fastest-growing part of the overall $12–20 billion pop record market.

Many of these "musicians" do not read music and don't know how to play anything but pop rock. Many have hearing-loss. Be ready to be surprised if you ever hear one of these groups play a "traditional" hymn *a la* rock. You haven't lived until you've heard *A Mighty Fortress Is Our God* at 90 decibels with a solid rock beat underneath and Mick Jagger-type male vocalist screaming the lyrics at the top of his lungs accompanied by a bluesy tenor-saxophone honkin' and snortin'.'

I felt like my brain was being fried. It was.

> More than one repetition of a musical phrase or lyric causes the music to become displeasing, and also causes a person to either enter a state of subconscious thinking (first stages of hypnosis) or it creates a state of irritation, anger. The human mind shuts down after three or four repetitions of a rhythm, melody, or harmonic progression. Further excessive repetitions cause people to *lose control of their thoughts. Rhythmic repetition in particular has been used universally by people, cults, religions, or social movements who are trying to push certain ethics through their music.*
>
> —Dr. Ballam, from *Music on the Brain* by Lawrence O'Donnell

Announcements

After about twenty to thirty minutes of "softening up" the audience (no longer a congregation) with loud rock music, we are finally given a respite. Usually an assistant pastor comes out and begins to mumble through the list of important social events taking place that week or in the near future. Traditionalists, like my wife and I, feel tired.

> There is a direct link between muscle strength and music. All the muscles in the body go weak when subject to the "stopped anapestic beat" (heavy backbeat of the rock drummer).
>
> —Dr. John Diamond, Australian physician, psychiatrist

Recently I began to see the similarities between a bullfight and a contemporary church service. Picadors are sent in to weaken and confuse the bull, so when the matador finally appears the bull is too weak to put up much of a fight.

In the announcements there is excitement over a coming Christian rock star, because the church is also a performance arena for those struggling bands that couldn't make it in mainstream rock music.

After the announcements we usually have the offering. At this point, some of us hope for just a few minutes of contemplative silence or soft background music to put us in a more worshipful mode after being whipped into an adrenal–driven frenzy by the mini rock concert we just experienced, but no, we are treated once more to more loud music while we search our billfolds and purses for cash. I would gladly pay any price by now to escape this torture chamber called modern-day "worship."

All through the first part of this show the volume of the music hovers between 80 and 105 decibels. This is no accident. Loud, repetitious music with a strong sharp backbeat of the drums does two things:

1. Loud music over-stimulates the adrenal glands, causing the listener to be forced into a heightened state of awareness (fight-or-flight response). This is usually mistaken for an outbreak of the Holy Spirit. Nothing could be further from the truth. Looks of sensual ecstasy, borderline erotic movements, closed eyes, hands and arms undulating overhead— all are supposed examples of deep expressions of worship.

2. The constant repetition tends to break down individual consciousness, forcing a unified group state-of-mind, and a favorite trick of most pagan religions and cults. Esalyn Institute in Carmel, California, uses similar techniques in their workshops for corporate executives.

Young parishioners eyes gleam with adrenaline-energy, faces are flushed from jumping, clapping, swaying, and singing (more like yelling) for twenty minutes or more. Now they are ready for the sermon, the message. Often at this moment we are all asked to turn to the person next to us and say something like, "Jesus loves you!" First names are exchanged and quickly forgotten, hands are shook, and we all have that warm and fuzzy feeling that comes with an adrenaline rush.

The Message

Most churches are envious today of the incredible success of the seeker–sensitive churches like Willow Brook and Rick Warren's Saddleback Church. Size has become more important than spiritually servicing those attending. Seeker-sensitive churches are very careful not to offend anyone. As a result, controversial topics like Heaven, Hell, sin, the blood, the virgin birth, Satan, spiritual warfare, Israel, coming judgment, etc., are saved for smaller groups, where they are often given a quick review and ignored. *Man's basic sinful nature and eternal judgment if not saved are downplayed or ignored.*

Salvation, when the alter call is given, seems more like an initiation into a social club than the deciding moment that determines where you will spend eternity.

The pastor is usually a young man (occasionally a woman) dressed casually who is immediately charming in manner, dress, and voice. Some Scripture is read, there is an exegesis (explanation), a wind up, and, occasionally, an altar-call. It's slick, short, often preceded by an even shorter mini-drama. If this pastor is on radio or television or knows Billy Graham or other big stars, he or she is even more looked up to or idolized.

Big Bucks

Big bucks can also be part of this picture. Leading television "evangelists" like *Oral and Richard Roberts, Benny Hinn, Robert Schuller, Jimmy Swaggert, TBN, CBN, Kenneth Copeland,* and a handful of others, average $5–75 million a year in income. No wonder these guys can wear silk Armani suits, fly private Lear jets, and live like kings. One of their favorite ploys is to ask people to send them money . . . and God will supposedly bless them by restoring ten times over what they sent the guy on television. Nice approach, but certainly not scriptural. *You cannot buy, bribe, or wheedle your way into Heaven.*

We are celebrity crazy today, both within and without the church. Of all places where being a celebrity is not important, it should be the church. There is only one big shot in Christianity and that is the Lord Himself. All the apostles made that clear in their epistles in the New Testament. All of us are sinners, saved by grace.

The Windup

Usually the pastor's message is twenty to thirty minutes long. There is a windup prayer, a benediction, and an exit. Sometimes we are blessed to exit without loud rock music; other times, the rock band has one last chance to over-stimulate our adrenal glands and numb our hearing.

Summary

Some churches have become palaces of entertainment. Our worship services have become like a television music review with a little Scripture thrown in. Those of us who want to find a quiet place to worship our God are having a harder and harder time finding it. Traditional hymns are thrown out without a thought. Casual carelessness is mistaken for warm friendliness. We are all dumbing down. This is not scriptural. This is not how the early church practiced the coming together of the saints.

In America today we have paganized Christianity to the point that the church of Corinth that Paul the apostle had to clean up in the Bible would seem conservative by comparison. God help us all unless we repent, stop trying for bigness, and start trying for holiness.

What Is Pagan Worship?

We use the style of music the majority of people in our church listen to on the radio. They like bright, happy, cheerful music *with a strong beat*. Their ears are accustomed to music with a *strong bass line and rhythm*. For the first time in history, there exists a universal music style that can be heard in every country of the world. Its called contemporary pop/rock.

—Rick Warren, *The Purpose Driven Church*, page 285

The Dynamic Duo

There you have it. The author of two of the most popular "Christian" books in modern times, *The Purpose Driven Life* and *The Purpose Driven Church*, with one fell swoop of his pen eliminates the barrier between sacred and secular music that has been in place for almost two thousand years.

Worship is for the Lord and His people. It isn't primarily for seekers, although we suddenly tame them into account. *Too many seeker-sensitive services have gutted the heart of worship.* I was in a mega-church in California and in the two Sundays I was there, there was hardly a reference to scripture. There were far more references to George Barna and George Gallup than to either the Bible or God.

—Oz Guinness: lecture at the CS Lewis Institute, 2002

Rick Warren learned to market Christianity from the guru of modern media and market-driven religion, Robert Schuller, of the Crystal Cathedral in Anaheim, California. . . the same Robert Schuller who said recently that he would be "proud" if his grandson became a Muslim. Warren says one of the reasons his church dumped all the hymns of the past two thousand years was because they were "elitist," and he openly boasts that the music in his church is "ear-splitting" in volume.

These two are among the wealthiest, most powerful Protestant religious leaders today. Both have trashed traditional church music, although Schuller holds on to some traditional hymns. Both lead huge churches, have millions of dollars in revenue, and both are without a clue as to the dangerous "wolves in sheep's clothing" they have turned loose not only in their churches but in a growing number of churches across America.

The rise of the Modern World through the Industrial Revolution (and later the electronic/atomic revolution) is so powerful, so pervasive and so pressurizing that you can barely get away from it. The world is so powerful today that what's surprising is there's almost *no world* denying branches of the Christian faith left."

—Oz Guinness, at CS Lewis Institute, 2002

Paganization of Worship

What is pagan worship? Pagan worship is the art or technique of worshipping other gods than *the God of the Bible*. Romans 1 describes the degeneration of man's worship from the worship of the Creator to the worship (through idols and images) of nature, man, and/or Satan under the guise of "other gods."

Secular Humanism

The twentieth century discovered and codified a new religion: the worship of "man." What we call secular humanism today is the elevation of the created to the status of the creator. This false premise is based on one of the many lies Lucifer, the "light bearer," used to deceive Eve in the Garden of Eden (Gen. 3).

Non-Biblical Worship

All non-biblical worship is pagan worship. Behind all the masks of the world's religions is the fallen one, Satan, who craves worship above everything else (Matt. 4). Over the many thousands of years of history since the flood of Noah, Satan has worked hard to pervert true worship to serve his own ends. He sends his demons to possess pagan worshippers, who then deceive many with "lying signs and wonders." Black magic, the occult, and all non-biblical "miracles," are deceiving manifestations of Satan designed to lead the innocent away from the one true God to the many false gods of a fallen world.

Spiritual Deception

Many pseudo-Christian religions misuse Scripture to deceive. They change the nature, purpose, and divinity of Jesus Christ into something else. With Christian Scientists and other metaphysical-based religions Christ becomes a non-personal "force" ("Let the force be with you") that can be manipulated by worshippers for selfish desires and goals.

Non-Biblical Jesus

With Mormons, Jesus becomes the "brother" of Satan. Both had a plan for man's salvation, but God chose Jesus' plan, thoroughly angering Satan, who set out to thwart Jesus' plan. With Jehovah's Witnesses, Jesus becomes a created being, a high order of angel like Michael, but not "divine" in the sense of being one with the godhead. Muslims believe Jesus was a prophet, and was divinely conceived, but did not die on the cross (Judas was the substitute) and that He, Jesus, will return someday to *destroy all Christians and Jews that have not converted to Islam* (the Hadith, the prophetic utterances of Islam).

The first objective of all pagan religions is to ignore or to deceive the believer regarding the Son of God. Muslims claim God never had a son; to a Christian Scientist, Jesus is a "force"; to a Buddhist, Jesus is a truly-realized human being; and to a Hindu, Jesus is just another avatar, a great spiritual leader that shows up every few thousand years or so to help straighten out mankind.

Loose Worship

The loose worship found in seeker-sensitive churches today claims an unhealthy and unholy secular intimacy with the godhead with songs that claim that Jesus can be your "buddy," your "main man," someone "nifty" and "cool." Drooling songs of not-too-subtly-hidden sexuality from pubescent females or long hair, bearded, nasal-droning, skinny "song leaders" are an offense to God, and to anyone who knows even the basics about the Bible and true Christian faith. Ear-splitting volume, sudden sharp sounds like a gun going off from the drummer, wailing sounds from the guitarist—like the siren of an ambulance—screaming, hippie-dressed singers mouthing monotonous pseudo–religious lyrics . . . all this is supposed to put you in a state of receptivity to worship?

I don't think so!

Arrogance

> So many pastors and pundits today are saying, "We've got to re-invent the church and get it moving forward—a new kind of Christian for the new kind of age." But when you look at the Scriptures and Christian history, *the church always goes forward by first going back.* What we're after is not re-inventing the church, but *reviving the Church.* And part of revival and reformation is *always going back to God's standards.*
>
> —Oz Guinness, CS Lewis Institute, 2002

Humility is supposed to be the number one virtue in the Bible; pride the number one sin . . . it was through pride that Satan rebelled and started all this hatred and spiritual deception we are still dealing with. When I read the books, listen to the music, and watch the sermons on television of these "modern" "seeker-sensitive" churches and their leaders, I see smugness, pride, arrogance, and incredible ignorance and naiveté regarding Satan and his ability to penetrate worship with his own agenda.

Imitation

Satan cannot create; he can only imitate or destroy. So many rituals in pagan worship are nothing but cheap imitations of the original, like those phony Rolex watches you can buy across the border. All the biblical events, places, holidays, and ceremonies related to worship are *twisted and perverted* into something else in pagan worship:

1. Animal sacrifice becomes child sacrifice among the Canaanites.
2. Celebration of the first-born becomes a tragedy when first-born are sacrificed rather than dedicated.
3. Ritual use of wine, representing the blood of Christ becomes actual "blood" in devil worship.
4. Music, used to elevate and lift the worshipper into a higher level of consciousness, becomes hypnotic, loud, repetitive, designed to take the worshipper into a group-collective consciousness at a lower level.
5. Dancing for joy becomes salacious, demonic, perverted.
6. Celebration of marriage between a man and a woman becomes celebration of marriage between those of a like sex.
7. Jewelry representing the dedication of the believer to God becomes occult symbols full of all kinds of demonic power (crystals, amulets, bracelets, etc.).
8. Raising the collective worship of believers to a higher level through the reading of Scripture and music becomes the lowering of consciousness through the hypnotic repetitions of pagan phrases and loud, syncopated rhythmic music.
9. Man worships in hopes of getting God's attention. Pagan worship hopes for demonic attention.
10. Denial of self in biblical Christianity becomes punishment of self in pagan worship, through flagellation (whips), cutting, etc.
11. Biblical worship elevates; pagan worship degrades. Pagan worship leaves man on a lower level than self-consciousness; biblical worship leaves one on a higher level.
12. True biblical worship is a little bit of Heaven; pagan worship is a peek into Hell.
13. Sexual energy is no longer suppressed and controlled, it is turned loose, lowering man to the level of a beast.
14. God wants to improve man's lot; Satan wants to degrade mankind.
15. God's desire is for man to love Him; Satan's desire is to teach mankind to hate the God of the Bible and His followers.

16. Alcohol and drugs are forbidden in biblical worship; they are often an essential part of pagan worship.

17. Special holidays honoring Christ and His ministry are celebrated annually. Pagan worship steals these holidays and turns them into something else. Christmas becomes "Saturnalia"; Resurrection Day becomes "Easter," the worship of the Canaanite sex-goddess Ashtar; All-Saints Day, celebrating the noble lives of those devoted to Christ, becomes "Halloween," dedicated to honoring the dark forces of the universe and so on.

In the carnal Christian church, many of these conflicting worship practices become entwined. Paul the apostle spent a large amount of his time in Corinth, a strong occult center in ancient Greece, in weaning the Corinthian church from carnal and pagan worship practices.

Today we face a similar problem to that of Paul. Our society has become largely pagan. How do we keep it out of the church? Why should we keep it out of the church? What is Satan's motivation in bringing in pagan practices to Christian worship? Why should we be on guard and check everything we do with Scripture to be sure that we are not being spiritually deceived.

Adolescent Rebellion

So much of the popular Christian rock music plays off the same natural tendencies of all teenagers to rebel against adult authority and tradition. We understand it in the world, but in the church *it is a different matter.* The Christian rock movement is also anti-fundamentalist, biblically illiterate (for the most part), and not under discipleship or submission to any reasonable authority.

Larry Norman, in his big "hit" (note: commercial success is considered to be most important) *Why Should the Devil Have All the Good Music,* trots out all the teenage rebellion themes: resistance to authority, long hair, desirous of loud music with a "beat" with which to worship. This song would be okay if it wasn't tied to worship. Traditional hymns are called "funeral marches." The singer rationalizes that Jesus would think this kind of rebellion to be "okay."

Is Pornography Next?

If we are going to let the world into the church, why not drop the bar another notch. Throughout history the combination of "worship" and sex has been potent. Most of the goddess religions that Judaism and Christianity replaced had an erotic base. Temple prostitutes were common, male and female.

I will argue the point with any "liberal" pastor or music and worship director that even *more* people will flock to their church if they have scantily-clad, attractive young ladies (and men) "read" Scripture from a see-through pulpit. My, oh my! Wouldn't church be "fun" then!

You may not realize it, but when Hugh Hefner started *Playboy* magazine, the first of a whole line of soft-core pornography magazines to emerge, he had illusions about the magazine being read for its "literature." Hugh hired some talented young writers to write for his magazine, but survey after survey revealed that young men bought his magazine for other reasons. Still, he did become big, wealthy, and attracted a lot of "readers" who might have at least rubbed elbows with good writing.

Couldn't we say the same? We could argue that although the soft-porn approach to Scripture reading might offend some "old fuddy-duddies," it certainly would enhance male attendance at church, and hopefully they would be able to filter out the gospel message from the carnal way of delivering it?

Rock is musical pornography. Changing the words to justify its admission to the sanctuary for worship services is just as indefensible as allowing soft porn into the sanctuary as well.

Hippie-led Extended Adolescence Churches

A sad commentary on the hippie movement of the '60s and the continued extended state of adolescence in this country is the fact that so many young people from the '60s on *did not want to grow up and be responsible for their own behavior.* This unwillingness to grow up has drifted into the church with former hippie pastors, music directors, and church leaders who now introduce this extended adolescence into the church. I've talked to the leaders of these churches—many of them are huge—and many have formed their own denomination around their extended adolescence ideas.

For instance in very large church of this type not to far from where we live, I interviewed the pastor and discovered: no one "joins" the church: the church government and definition of job authority and responsibility is casual at best; there is no dress code; musicians can pretty much play what they want as loud as they want; and there is a fuzziness regarding fiscal responsibilities and a resistance to criticism or suggestion.

They're okay and smug in their culturally-adapted Jesus. They've managed to hang on to their teenage persona while surrounding it with Scripture out of context and a great emphasis on emotion and works. I have found that usually one person is totally in charge . . . and whatever this person says goes. That too is non-biblical.

Willowbrook

Now with the phenomenal success of the "seeker-sensitive" churches like Willowbrook and the best-selling Purpose Driven books of Rick Warren, mainline conservative churches are dropping their traditional services all over the country and adopting this new type of service and music in mass. *They are making a tragic mistake and will live to regret it.* I believe this church is totally insensitive to the fact that they are driving away many older parishioners who cannot stand the music or the rock festival atmosphere of worship.

Major Christian rock artists come through, playing a song or two in service and giving a concert at night. The tables outside the sanctuary are loaded with this artist's latest CDs, DVDs, bios, etc.

I feel like I'm back in high school when I visit their campus. I know the senior pastor at a large "seeker-sensitive" rock music church. He's a friendly fellow and a good teacher of the Bible. However, he was not interested *one bit* in reading my book *Crisis in Christian Music* when it came out, even out of curiosity (and I gave him a free copy), or my offer to start a choir for a more "blended" service for those who couldn't handle the loud guitars and the repetitious, childish songs presented to the congregation in worship.

Trends

Surprisingly, there are a growing number of young Christians who are detoxing themselves from the addiction of "Christian rock" and secular rock (see the chapter on "By Their Fruits Ye Shall Know Them") and are beginning to demand a more serious, traditional, and scriptural sound worship service.

So many members [today] of the younger generation want history, liturgy, and richness [in worship] again. They're going back to the early church fathers and the Scriptures. *They want the cross, tradition, and worship.* The people who cut out all that stuff in the name of relevance have suddenly found themselves washed up.

—Oz Guinness, CS Lewis Institute, 2002

John Steinbeck

I'm struck by the contrast between the slick, theater-like churches of the "seeker-sensitive" crowd and the traditional, smaller churches, where worship meant something more than entertainment and self-glorification. No one captures the difference better than one of America's greatest writers, John Steinbeck. The excerpt below if from one of his last books, *Travels with Charlie*, pages 70–71:

Sunday morning, in a Vermont town, my last day in New England, I shaved, dressed in a suit, polished my shoes, whited my sepulcher and looked for a church to attend. Several I eliminated for reason I do not now remember, but on seeing a John Knox church I drove into a side street and parked Rocinante [his RV] out of sight, gave Charlie [his dog] his instructions about watching the truck, and took my way with dignity to a church of blindingly white ship lap. I took my seat in the rear of the spotless, polished place of worship. The prayers were to the point, directing the attention of the Almighty to certain weaknesses and undivine tendencies I know to be mine and could only suppose were shared by others gathered there.

The service did my heart and I hope my soul some good. It had been long since I had heard such an approach. It is our practice now, at least in the large cities, to find from our psychiatric priesthood that our sins aren't really sins at all but accidents that are set in motion by forces beyond our control. There was no such nonsense in this church. The minister, a man of iron with tool-steel eyes and a delivery like a pneumatic drill, opened up with prayer and reassured us that we were a pretty sorry lot.

And he was right! We didn't amount to much to start with, and due to our own tawdry efforts we had been slipping ever since. Then, having softened us up, he went into a glorious sermon, a fire-and-brimstone sermon. Having proved that we, or perhaps only I, were no damn good, he painted with cool certainty what was likely to happen to us if we didn't make some basic reorganizations for which he didn't hold out much hope. He spoke of hell as an expert, not the mush-mush hell of these soft days, but a well-stoked, white-hot hell served by technicians of the first order.

This reverend brought it to a point where we could understand it, a good hard coal fire, plenty of draft, and a squad of oven-hearth devils who put their hearts into their work and their work was me. I began to feel good all over. For some years now God has been a pal to us, practicing togetherness, and that causes the same emptiness a father does by playing softball with his son. But this Vermont God cared enough about me to go to a lot of trouble kicking the hell out of me. He put my sins in a new perspective.

Whereas they had been small and mean and nasty and best forgotten, this minister gave them some size and bloom and dignity. I hadn't been thinking very well of my self for some years, but if my sins had this dimension there was some pride left. I wasn't a naughty child but a first rate sinner, and I was going to catch it.

I felt so revived in spirit that I put five dollars in the plate, and afterward, in front of the church, shook hands warmly with the minister and as many of the congregation as I could. It gave me a lovely sense of evil-doing that lasted clear through till Tuesday. I even considered beating Charley to give him some satisfaction too, because Charley is only a little less sinful than I am. All across the country I went to church on Sundays, a different denomination every week, but nowhere did I find the quality of the Vermont preacher. He forged a religion designed to last, no predigested obsolescence.

Acceptable Worship

Definition of Acceptable Worship

According the *Webster's New World Dictionary* (2nd ed. Simon/Schuster, 1986), worship means:

1. Reverent devotion to a deity.
2. Religious homage and veneration.
3. A church service or rite.
4. Extreme devotion, intense love and admiration
5. Greatness of character, honor, dignity, worthiness.
6. Adore and venerate a deity.
7. An act of religious devotion

Nowhere in this definition do I find the word "entertainment," "casualness," "seeker-sensitive," or "worldliness." How far have many of our churches moved from the original definition? The guidebook for everything we do in our spiritual lives is the Bible.

Guidebook

Is there a guidebook for "acceptable" worship? There sure is! It's called *The Bible*.

Proper worship should be of a holy, omniscient, omnipresent, eternal being who made everything: man, earth, all that is on or in the earth, the planets, the universe, the invisible world, the plan of salvation, an eventual sin-free new Heaven and new earth—our God *is* a mighty God, beyond our human mind's ability to comprehend. However, we can and should realize three things about our relationship to God:

1. Man and the present earth is under a curse because of sin and eventually will be destroyed and all mankind judged.

2. There is a way of avoiding this fate. John 3:16 says: "For God so loved the world that he gave his only begotten Son that whoever believes in him should not perish but have everlasting life." Confessing and repenting of your sins is the first step. The second step is accepting Jesus Christ as your Lord and Savior. That means surrendering total control of your body, your mind, and your soul to the Holy Spirit that comes to dwell within the heart of every true believer.

3. Those that sincerely fulfill (to the best of their ability) the qualifications given in the second example will become part of the "body" of Christ, the "bride" of Christ and will rule and reign with Him on earth (after the Tribulation) and in Heaven (the New Jerusalem described in Rev. 22)

4. Those that reject the free gift of salvation will spend an eternity separated from Him and from all good and lovely things . . . a place of darkness.

Philosophy of Worship
Again, following biblical worship principles all acceptable worship:

1. Recognizes the awesome, exclusive and total power of the God of the Bible *and no other.*

2. The total helplessness and hopelessness of unregenerate man; man without Christ.

3. Heaven cannot be attained through good works, sacrifices, or complicated worship, but only through the acceptance of Jesus Christ and the repentance of sin.

4. The centerpiece of any worship service is God Himself. *We do not attend worship services to be entertained, cajoled, celebrate fellowship, or to receive homilies "about" the Bible. Our primary purpose for being there is to offer worship from our sin-stained hands and lips to a Holy God.*

5. Music's purpose in worship is to edify, unify, and drive out the evil forces that may be present by lifting up the name of our Savior and Redeemer in song. The musicians are not entertainers or "artists." They are priests, assisting in the worship service dedicated to a holy, forgiving, loving God.

6. After achieving the first goal, the primary lifting up of our sin-stained hands to a holy God who has allowed us to have eternal fellowship with Him through the sacrifice of His Son on the cross, the second goal is to hear the Word of God from a pure translation of the Bible. The proper attitude for a congregation is to stand when the Word of God is being read. *Scripture reading should be no shorter than one chapter or psalm.* A series of short scriptures taken out of contexts is always dangerous. When that happens, any message can be twisted and supported from the Bible. *That is the primary reason we have hundreds of different Christian denominations.* Their "founders" took certain scriptures out of context, built a doctrine around it, and separated themselves from the greater body of Christ. Satan is always trying to separate the body of Christ, and he's done a good job of it through scripture twisting.

7. The pastor's responsibility is to do an exegesis on the scripture that has been read: to explain it's deeper meanings, how to apply the principles outlined in our daily lives, and how it relates to other scriptures. Ideally, the pastor should be working through an entire book of the Bible and should not ignore more difficult to understand Old Testament books. *God has them there for a reason and God holds us responsible for knowing His Word.*

8. Prayer is the third priority in a worship service. Oh, how we all need prayer! We need to pray to God for forgiveness of sin (1 John 1:9). We need to pray for those in our congregation who are going through severe trials. We need to pray for fellow Christians around the world, many of whom are undergoing severe persecution. We need to pray for the pastoral and church staff, the president of the United States, and all our elected officials. We need to pray for our unsaved friends and loved ones. And we need to pray for Jesus to come back soon for His Church. This kind of prayer cannot be accomplished in the usual one or two minutes given in today's service for prayer. Also, there needs to always be a period of silent prayer, where each of us can pray as the Holy Spirit leads us.

9. Communion should be offered at least once a month. Proper scriptures regarding communion should be read. *Non-believers or those living "out of fellowship" (in sin) should be cautioned not to take communion.* Those are biblical rules, not mine

10. An offering is allowable, but it should be done in dignity with lifting, appropriate music being played softly during the offertory. The offertory usually occurs just before the scripture reading or after the sermon.

11. The plan of salvation should *always be given* along with an offer to meet with anyone who just gave his or her life to Christ, as well as an offer to meet after the service with any in need of special prayer.

12. Announcements should be printed in the bulletin. Special announcements must be made *before* the official "worship" service begins. The same is true for introduction of staff, visiting dignitaries or missionaries, directors of special projects, etc. Baptisms should be part of the service, before the reading of scripture. Congregations should be cautioned that once they enter the sanctuary for a worship service all talking, whispering, etc., should cease. Focus on getting yourselves ready for worship. Fellowship, which is very important, should occur on the patio before and after services.

Regarding the presentation of music in a worship service:

1. No drums or amplified instruments (electric guitar, bass, synthesizer)
2. All musicians dressed appropriately: no jeans or rock-group gear.
3. The lyrics of selections to be scripturally based, or appropriate to the sermon-topic. No "Jesus is my kind of guy!" lyrics.
4. Volume should be kept at medium and certainly below 60–70 decibels.
5. Musical selections, except for the prelude and postlude to be kept short.
6. Applause should be discouraged. The musicians are not there to perform or receive accolades from the congregation (or sell CDs). They are there to assist in worship.
7. All musicians need to be told by their leader before every worship service that they are not performers but priests . . . and the music they make is an offering to Jesus Christ. They are to play and sing "as unto Him," not the people in the congregation.

This kind of service does not preclude the use of contemporary Christian music. However, it cannot have a rock base or accompaniment, and must meet the other standards regarding lyrics, volume, and style. *There should be a balance between standard hymns and praise songs and newer material.*

Love Not the World

The world and everything it stands for is under judgment. It's just a matter of time.

Look around you. Everything you see, including the planet, will someday be purified by fire and made sin-free (Rev. 22). It is so easy to let the world sneak into our church services. Radio and in particular television ministries have been partially to blame; television demands "entertainment," and so these ministries cater to that need. In the process they have contaminated and weakened their worship services, albeit to reach a wider audience, but at what cost?

Outline

Below is an example of an outline of a proper worship service:

- Prelude (piano or organ, or solo wind or string instrument): 5–10 minutes
- Announcements: 1–3 minutes
- Congregational singing (traditional hymn or appropriate praise song)
- Opening prayer (from scripture): 3–5 minutes
- Congregational singing
- Baptisms, presentation of new members
- Reading of Scripture (all stand): 5–10 minutes
- Congregational singing
- Offertory (appropriate soft, uplifting music): 3–5 minutes
- Sermon: 20–30 minutes
- Communion (when offered)
- Closing prayer: 1–3 minutes
- Postlude (piano or organ, or solo wind or string instrument): 3–5 minutes

I believe there is a hunger on the part of those who are of the body of Christ to return to a pure, holy, respectful worship. Evangelical crusades and efforts are noble, but should be kept separate from worship services. Even then, the unbeliever must not be allowed to think it is okay with God for him to keep his worldly music and other passions that conflict with spiritual growth. Quantity has never impressed God. Quality always has been important. Finally, Scripture should be the final arbiter in all disagreements about how to present a worship service, not public opinion, surveys, polls, or some hot new book selling sloppy *agape*.

The Early Church (A.D. 33–350)

Welcome to the early church. We meet in homes and out-of-the-way places. We never know when the government will turn on us and persecute us. Although we are usually model citizens, they are suspicious of us and what we stand for. Spiritual freedom eventually manifests itself in individual freedom or representative government. Slaves have no rights. Jesus gives them the same status as the freeborn, hence the fear of the Roman patrician class.

Slaves

There are so many slaves in the Roman Empire—they estimate fifteen to twenty slaves in Rome itself for every free-born (patrician) Roman. This new faith, where all class, race, and gender barriers are broken down, is like a fresh breeze to the oppressed. Accepting Jesus Christ, *Christos*, as their Lord and Savior, along with the promise of forgiveness of sin as well as the promise of a glorious afterlife is particularly appealing to the Roman slaves, for it promises a far better life in the next world than their present circumstances.

However, there is a bonus in a slave becoming a follower of Christ. They are now under the obligation of obeying their masters and must not cheat or lie to them. Many slave owners have noticed a sudden change in character in their slaves when they become Christians.

Slaves to Sin

This new faith teaches that those who have not surrendered their lives to Jesus Christ are slaves to Satan and sin, no matter how highborn and free in society they may be. Only Christ can bring true freedom, true joy, true peace, and true relief from carrying around the burden of sin we all carry . . . until we surrender it to Christ and it is nailed to the cross forever.

The joy of the Christian martyrs in the arena who sing hymns and psalms and have looks of ecstasy on their faces while being attacked by wild animals was a startling wake-up call to the average Roman. How can you fake this kind of bliss when going through the most horrendous of deaths? Many Romans leave the arenas pondering the power of this new faith and often secretly begin investigating it on their own.

Hierarchy

Yes, our church is organized. We have a pastor, an assistant pastor, elders, and deacons. Each member of our congregation knows their spiritual gifts and they try to practice them as often as possible. The early church is totally dependent on three things for spiritual guidance: prayer, the Word of God (the Holy Bible), and the power of the Holy Spirit working through our leaders and the congregation.

We are probably the most democratic organization on the planet. Christ said in His Revelation that He hates the doctrine of the Nicolaitians, Nico meaning "above," and laity meaning "the congregation." There are no big shots here. There is church discipline, but it is administered with love through the prayerful meetings of the elders, the deacons, and the congregation.

Christ's death on the cross removed the need for any intercessor in man's quest for intimate fellowship with God. True Christian believers can enter the "holy of holies" of God's presence without any intercessor—save the sacrifice of Christ on the cross, and the truly repentant heart of the believer.

Counseling

Those who need counseling and guidance will meet with selected elders or deacons. *Men never counsel women; women never counsel men.* All information revealed in a counseling session is confidential. The Scriptures, the Holy Word of God, is the final guideline and decision-maker in all counseling and church discipline situations.

We search the scriptures for answers, for we believe *everything* we need to know about organizing a church, leading worship service, teaching, and counseling are found somewhere in Scripture. The wonderful prophecy of the coming Messiah in Isaiah 9:6–9 confirms this belief:

> For unto us a child is born, unto us a son is given: and the government shall be upon his shoulder: and his name shall be called *Wonderful, Counsellor,*

*The mighty God, The everlasting Father, The Prince of Peace. Of the increase
of his government and peace there shall be no end, upon the throne of
David, and upon his kingdom, to order it, and to establish it with judgment
and with justice from henceforth even for ever. The zeal of the LORD of
hosts will perform this.*

—Isaiah 9:6–7

Scripture

The Bible is our survival manual. We only have manuscripts that have been
hand-copied and handed down secretly and with great care from the time of
the resurrection of our Lord and Savior, Jesus Christ (A.D. 33) until now. Our
Old Testament Scriptures were borrowed and copied from the local Jewish synagogue, for their tradition of carefully handing down the Scriptures
through thoroughly trained scribes has never been equaled.

We imitate the Jewish scribes in carefully copying the four Gospels, the
Book of Acts, the epistles of Paul, James, John, Peter, and Jude, and the final
Revelation from Jesus Christ Himself.

Bible Classes

In our Bible classes, we study the revealed truth from the time of Christ until
the completion of the Book of Revelation. These new spiritual truths we call
the *New Testament*. Participation in Bible classes is a must for all members
of our little band of believers. First we study the basic essentials of our faith,
finalized in something called the Apostle's Creed. Then a careful study of the
four Gospels, followed by the thrilling story of the very early church outlined
in the Book of Acts, the many letters or epistles, and finally the final revealed
Word of God in the Book of Revelation.

Old Testament

The Old Testament begins with a careful study of Genesis, followed by the
Psalms, the Proverbs, the Pentateuch (first five books of the Bible), the po-
etic books (Song of Solomon, Esther, Ruth), the Major Prophets (Isaiah,
Jeremiah, Ezekiel, Daniel), and the Minor Prophets. *We look for Jesus Christ
on every page and we look for prophetic guidelines that tell us how to worship, how
to pray, how to live, how to protect ourselves and our family, and what Heaven,
Hell, and Jesus are like.*

One of the criteria for becoming a deacon, elder, or pastor is a deep knowledge and understanding of Holy Scripture.

Joining Our Church

Anyone is welcome to attend our church, for we are all sinners, saved by the blood of the Lamb, but it is not easy to join our church. We are careful to make sure that all those who wish to join are leading (to the best of their ability) godly lives, are taking care of their family, and are biblically literate. Usually a probationary period of two years is demanded, followed by some tests, and finally a confession of faith in front of the entire congregation along with *completely renouncing the works of the devil in our previous lives.*

Baptism

Baptism usually follows—as an act of faith and as a symbol of total submission to Jesus Christ. Full immersion is the common practice, and usually baptisms are held at a local stream or lake. Those being baptized have an opportunity to share with the congregation who they were before Christ and who the hope to be after salvation.

We do not practice infant baptism. Baptism, like salvation, is a voluntary act and cannot be symbolically applied to a child or forced on someone who is not ready.

We do dedicate our children to Christ, sprinkle water on them as a symbol of the protection of the Holy Spirit, and ask the family in front of the congregation to pledge that they will, to the best of their ability, raise their child in a godly home. The congregation then pledges to support the family in this endeavor.

Marriage

Marriage is a sacred institution, symbolizing the eventual marriage of Jesus Christ to His Bride, the church. It is not to be taken lightly; the church will not marry a couple when one is not a believer. Several sessions or meetings are held with the pastor, the bride often with the lady deacons. The pastors, elders, and deacons vote on approving a marriage ceremony. Often, couples are counseled to wait until they have a better understanding of Scripture, the plan of salvation, and the responsibilities of the wife to the husband and vice versa.

Funerals

To a Christian, dying is graduation. When people left this earth in the Old Testament, the prophets and scribes tell us that they "died." When someone who knows Christ leaves this earth in the New Testament, it is said that they are "asleep." Every believer knows that when they die they are instantly in the arms of Jesus Christ. As a consequence, funerals are looked upon as graduation ceremonies and more of an opportunity for celebration than for tears. The tears are only for those who are still on this planet and who not yet graduated. Their bodies will be resurrected at a sudden event called the Rapture (1 Cor. 15:15–end; 1 Thess. 4).

Services

We meet to worship God usually on Saturday or Sunday evenings. The lady deacons provide childcare. Services can be as short as forty-five minutes or as long as three hours. The typical outline of our services would have been:

Opening Prayer. Opening Prayers are short and usually from Scripture. We are not tolerant of long-winded, self-composed opening prayers.

Pagan Music. We are very careful to distinguish our music from the type of music often heard at pagan ceremonies. Pagan worship is almost always accompanied by loud, syncopated music. Pagan music is loud, sensual, with a lot of drums; the lyrics are usually short and repetitive. Pagan worship uses music to (1) activate human sexuality and self-hypnosis, and (2) put the listener into a semi-trance so demonic forces can enter their minds to temporarily or in some extreme instances totally control them. Their music is loud, frenzied, sensual, syncopated, and repetitive, and becomes like a drug, with the listener entranced, enthralled, and under control of the forces of darkness.

In pagan worship the repetitive rhythms of the music is used to call forth demonic spirits, put the worshippers in a state of trance, and activate sensual and emotional feelings that become difficult to control. Pagan music often causes the listeners to cut themselves, much as the priests of Baal did in the showdown with Elijah in the Bible at the battle on Mt. Carmel between the God of Israel and the pagan god Baal (1 Kings 19).

Church Music. The music in our church is offered up to God. Singers and instrumentalists do not perform for the congregation or the pastoral staff. They sing and play as unto God. Music serves several purposes in our church. Its primary purpose is to drive away those demonic forces that always hang around a Christian religious service, hoping to cause some sort of distraction, disturbance, or general boredom. When we lift the name of our Lord and Savior in song, *it drives away the demonic forces.* This way the following scriptural reading and pastoral exegesis (explanation and expansion on the scripture read) *goes to the heart, not just the head.*

Songs. Songs are sung unaccompanied or accompanied by a hand-held harp or a guitar-like string instrument. We cannot afford an organ. Besides, the organ is associated with events in the Roman Coliseum or arena—places where many of our brothers or sisters have died for their faith. I doubt if the organ will ever be accepted as a proper musical instrument for a Christian worship service. Our congregation is discouraged from clapping for a soloist or a group of musicians. We do not want people coming to our church for a performance or to be entertained. We want them to come to worship the one true God and His Son Jesus Christ.

We prayerfully consult our guide, the Holy Spirit, for guidance in selecting music, prayers, and sermon topics.

Summary

We are the church of Jesus Christ. We submit to the will of the Holy Spirit. We do not allow in word or deed anything that is contradictory to Scripture or to the guidance of the Holy Spirit. Our aim is be humble servants of the one true God, Jesus Christ, and pray for the salvation of others.

Yes, we want all men to come to know Jesus, to be born again, but we do not and will not be tempted to use worldly means and ways to attract sinners. Unless the Holy Spirit brings them, their salvation will be temporary at best, as pointed out by our Savior in the parable of the sower in Matthew 13.

Music is used to unify the body in worship, to drive away evil spirits, and to glorify our God. It is not entertainment. Its purpose is also to teach Scripture through song. The individual singer or accompanist are just tools in the hands of God, and should receive no more glory and appreciation than the gardener that plants the flowers outside our sanctuary.

A Brief History of Church Music

Until the 1960s in the USA, the church had its music and the world had its music. Church music was called "sacred" and the world's music was called "secular." No one expected to hear secular music in church. Seldom did one hear sacred music in bars, dance halls, theaters, or soundtracks to movies. The two were separate. Everyone understood that . . . until the 1960s.

Old Testament. Music is not mentioned often in the Bible (see the chapter on music and the Bible), but when it is, it is usually in a supportive role. There are many songs in the Bible: the Song of Miriam (Moses' sister), sung in victory after the Red Sea swallowed up the pursuing army of Egypt; the songs that David sang to soothe the depressing demon sent to harass Saul; the fact that the Psalms themselves are really songs, often with instructions on how they were to be accompanied.

Tribal Societies and Music. Like all tribal societies, there were songs to celebrate birth, adolescence, courtship, marriage, lullabies for babies, death, special holidays, victory in battle, seasons of the year, and humorous, entertaining, and dance songs. Sometimes great battles, natural disasters, or great tragedies were preserved through songs.

Greek and Roman. Religious music for the Greek and later Roman religions generally fell into two categories: either raucous, loud, boisterous, sensual and repetitive—the music of Bacchus, the god of wine; or soft, very melodic, and inspirational songs—celebrating the quieter gods like Apollo.

The Early Church (A.D. 32–320). The early church was the persecuted church. Services were held mostly in homes, sometimes in natural surroundings, like the catacombs outside of Rome. Music was used to unify and elevate the body of believers through song, drive away evil spirits through the lifting up of the name of Jesus Christ, emphasize the message, teach Scripture, and glorify God. It was not used to entertain, fill in, or glorify the performers.

Most songs were simple; most were taken from Scripture and usually sung without accompaniment. If accompanied, the instruments were often the hand-held harp or the flute. The music was not loud, repetitious, danceable, sensual, or hypnotic.

Pagan vs. Christian. Pagan songs were loud, repetitive, syncopated, used a lot of drums, and were mostly accompanied by a wide variety of instruments. Early Christian music was usually soft, non-repetitive, and seldom accompanied—sung a cappella. The early church was constantly on the lookout for attempts on the part of Satan to infiltrate their worship and compromise it. Most instrumental music was considered sensual, emotional, and was associated with the secular entertainment centers of the time: the circus, the theater, the amphitheater, the coliseum, and entertainment for raucous banquets and orgies.

The Organ. A fascinating historical footnote is the fact that the organ, the oldest of the keyboard instruments was not used in the church until it was introduced into worship by Pope Vitalian in A.D. 570. The churches were getting so large, only the powerful pipes of the organ and brass instruments were strong enough to lead worship. One of the reasons for not using the organ sooner was its bloody association with the gladiatorial games in the arena, where many early Christians died as well. The organ was used in the arena to announce each event and to heighten the excitement of the mob.

The organ caught on because of its power to fill the increasingly larger churches, as well as the simplicity of its operation (bellows filled with air were routed to pitched pipes via the keyboard of the organist). By the tenth century Germany and England were both manufacturing organs.

The Cromwellian Revolution in England in the early eighteenth century saw a return to unaccompanied church music. At that time, zealots destroyed many of the organs in the churches in England with axes. Later, the French Revolution (1789) saw wanton destruction of hundreds of French harpsichords (early keyboard instrument) but not for religious reasons.

Greek Orthodox. The Greek Orthodox (Eastern) Church continued in the tradition of a cappella singing. Consequently, musical instruments to this day are not to be found in most Greek or Russian Orthodox churches.

Tenth Century. By the late tenth century, musical instruments saw limited use throughout the churches of France, Germany, Spain, and the British

Isles. Common instruments used in church music of the time included the organ, psaltery, harp, lute, viol, and horn.

A Comparison. Pagan songs were metrical (strong accented rhythms in double or triple time), while early Christian music was often non–metrical (Gregorian chants). The church even looked on the tambourine (a small hand-held drum with bangles on the side and long associated with lively Jewish worship) with suspicion for many centuries.

The early church believed the human voice to be a "living" means by which God was glorified by each worshipper joining in song. Musical instruments were lifeless, man-made creations without a soul, hence ignored for centuries in church music. Some churches and early church leaders actually banned the use of musical instruments in worship. The Gregorian chant was to elevate the worshipper toward God, not to entertain him or the congregation. Canon 97 of the *Synod of Basil* (c. 400) mentions that solo artistry was of no concern to God.

> Niceta of Reminesia believed that instrumental music belonged to the childhood state of the Hebrew people. Unaccompanied singing was thought a higher form of praise that lifted the Christian *closer to God*. . . . Basil the Great considered all musical instruments analogous with the "passions of the flesh," except for the psaltery [early primitive keyboard instrument].
> —Edward Dickinson, *Music in the History of the Western Church*
> (London: Oxford Press, 1967), page 55

Constantine. When the Christian church became the state religion under the leadership of the Roman emperor Constantine after A.D. 320, the early church was combined with pagan religions that traced their roots back to ancient Babylon. Many changes took place. A professional clergy took over the church; a professional choir and church musicians emerged; and music was used to create wonder, awe, and often hypnotic-like trances through constant repetition in the new, stain-glassed cathedrals.

The Reformation. Martin Luther was a musician. He earned his way through law school playing lute and singing bawdy ballads in beer halls. After the birth of the Protestant church, he wrote Christian lyrics to some of these tavern melodies. When questioned about this practice, he supposedly replied, "Why should the devil have all the good tunes!" However, Luther

had a healthy respect for the power of music and kept pagan musical practices out of the sanctuary and the worship service.

Music and the Bible

Because the Bible is the word of God, we should read it like no other book, on our knees in great humility before him. But because the Bible is also the words of men, we should read it like every other book, applying our minds diligently to its study.

—John Stott

Some day those of us who are truly Christians will be taken up suddenly from this planet in an event the Bible calls the Rapture. We suddenly find ourselves (like the apostle John) before the throne of God (Rev. 4–5). There is much singing, rejoicing, and lifting of hands. Suddenly, the curtain behind the throne of God parts, smoke rises, and behind the smoke . . . a giant Christian rock band, with long-haired screaming singers dressed in leather pants, grotesque makeup, earrings, and tattoos. Huge amplifiers pump ear-splitting animal-like sounds from the guitar. The singer with pink hair is jumping up and down, screaming "Jesus, Jesus!"

Sorry, for those who champion rock music in the church. That's a vision that I don't think you will ever see. *If you do, you'd better check with someone as to where you are. It may not be Heaven.*

Perversion

To pervert something is to destroy, camouflage, or compromise its original purpose.

Music in the church and in the Bible has for the most part been used to (1) glorify God, and (2) unify the brotherhood of believers. One of the greatest victories of Satan in the past fifty years has been his ability to convince musicians, pastors, elders, deacons, priests, and congregations that rock music belongs in a worship service.

Fulfillment of Prophecy

In Revelation 2–3 Christ evaluates the seven churches, which were literal churches but were also models for the changes the church went through in the almost two thousand years of Christian worship. The last two churches, the church of Philadelphia and the church of Laodicea, are models of contrasting contemporary churches in the latter days—the times we are presently living in.

Church of Philadelphia

The church of Philadelphia was the church of "brotherly love," this church Christ compliments for its steadfastness in upholding the sanctity of the Gospel and for their evangelical and missionary efforts. Christ promises this church that it will not go through the time of testing that will "come upon the whole world," in other words the Tribulation.

Church of Laodicea

On the other hand, the Laodicean church—rich, prideful, full of itself—is warned that because it is neither "hot" (on fire for the Lord) or "cold" (legalistic but scriptural, like the church of Ephesus) that it would be spewed from Christ's mouth, symbolically saying that *that* type of church could not and would not be part of the body of Christ until it was disciplined for its pride, sensuality, and worldliness.

Every Christian believer today must choose between these two types of churches. There is no third choice. To stay with the worldly Laodicean church is to risk God's wrath and discipline and possibly endure part or all of the terrible historical period of the future the Bible calls the Tribulation.

All Things Bright and Beautiful

Yes, there will be music in Heaven; no, it will not be Christian rock. There is no scriptural support for that belief, and common sense alone should tell us that that's not true. Heaven is where everything is clean, bright, beautiful, loving, kind, gentle, spiritual, not sensual, where we glorify God, not man. None of the above characteristics describe Christian rock music.

What Does the Bible Say About Music?

The first mention of music chronologically in the scriptures is Job 38:7:

When the morning stars sang together, and all the sons of God [angels]
shouted for joy?

And his brother' name was *Jubal:* he was the father of all such as handle
the harp and organ.

—Genesis 4:21

In the original *Hebrew, kinnar* is a generic word for *all* string instruments.
Ugab is the generic word for *all* wind instruments (usually translated as flute,
pipe, and organ). Note carefully that Jubal is of the lineage of Cain, and Cain
was driven away from his genealogical family because he killed his brother.
Genesis 5 introduces another genealogical line that is through Adam and
then through Seth, God's replacement for Cain.

And Miriam the prophetess, the sister of Aaron, took a timbrel [*toph*] in
her hand; and all the women went out after her with timbrels [*tophs*] and
with dances. And Miriam answered them, Sing ye to the LORD, for he
hath triumphed gloriously; the horse and his rider hath he thrown into
the sea.

—Exodus 15:20–21

This is the first song in the Bible. It celebrates the destruction of Pharaoh's
army by the waves of the Red Sea when they attempt to cross and trap the
escaping Jewish slaves under Moses. Bible scholars estimate that Miriam was
at this point in her life in her late eighties (Exod. 2:7, 7:7). Great joy accompanied by *light* percussion and dancing illustrates the importance of music to
Jewish cultural life. Note: They had their tambourines with them and read-
ily available! That tells us two things: music and dance were important and
secondly, *they anticipated this victory.*

Final note: This was *not* a sacred worship service; this was a celebration
of a great military victory brought on by God's grace. Consequently, singing
and dancing were not only permitted *but encouraged.* Throughout the Bible
we will find a consistency regarding the type and style of music for worship,
for celebrations, for battle, etc.

Today's church musicians would be wise to adhere to these guidelines.

And it came to pass on the third day in the morning, that there were thunders and lightnings, and a thick cloud upon the mount, and the voice of the trumpet [*shofar*] exceeding loud; so that all the people that was in the camp *trembled*.

—Exodus 19:16

God, not man, made this musical sound. It was loud because of the awesome presence of the Holy One. Some of you may remember the scene in the Steven Speilberg movie *Close Encounters of the Third Kind* when American scientists tried to communicate with a giant descending spacecraft through musical notes. The UFO answered with a voice so powerful it shattered all the glass in the buildings and cars near the site. Such was the scene at Mt. Sinai.

For the first and last time God speaks to an entire people in the Bible. God originally spoke the Ten Commandments to all the Jews. The awesome power of His voice so frightened the Jewish people that they begged Moses to tell God to not do it again, to only speak through His prophet Moses: "Then they said to Moses, You speak with us and we will hear; but let not God speak with us, lest we die" (Exod. 20:19).

Make thee two trumpets [*hsosra*] of silver; of a whole piece shalt thou make them: that thou mayest use them for the calling of the assembly, and for the journeying of the camps.

—Numbers 10:2

This is the first mention of hand-crafted trumpets as opposed to the ram's horn *shofar*. From here on, both types of trumpets are frequently mentioned. According to the Jewish historian Josephus (*Antiquities*, 3:12.6), these trumpets were approximately eighteen inches long, slender, straight pipes with flared openings at one end. The triumphal Arch of Titus in Rome, celebrating the defeat of the Jews by the Romans in A.D. 70, in bas-relief actually shows the trumpets captured as war booty and brought back to Rome along with the temple menorah and other religious and worship objects.

Man-made trumpets were made out of silver and were used for signaling because the sound they generated carried long distances. Long blasts were used to assemble the Jews of the Exodus to the tent of meeting and worship and later were used to announce certain religious feasts. They were also used in battle and to signal community movement. Generally these "blasts" were short, repetitive, and staccato. Note: These trumpets were to be played by priests, never by laymen.

> Let our lord now command thy servants, which are before thee, to seek out a man, who is a cunning player on an harp [lyre, or *kinnar* (Heb.]: and it shall come to pass, when the evil spirit from God is upon thee [Saul], that he shall play with his hand, and thou shalt be well. And Saul said unto his servants, Provide me now a man that can play well, and bring him to me. Then answered one of the servants, and said, Behold, I have seen a son of Jesse the Bethlehemite, that is cunning in playing, and a mighty valiant man, and a man of war, and prudent in matters, and a comely person, and *the LORD is with him.*
>
> —1 Samuel 16:16–18

This is the first documented case of treating mental illness or possession with music. Note that David is able to soothe the troubling spirit not because he is a skilled musician, which he was, but because *the Lord was with Him.*

Today's church musicians take note: Your musical skills are just one part of the dimension of your important ministry. Unless the *Lord is with you,* you will not be able to drive the troubling spirits that descend on every congregation when they go to worship.

> And it came to pass, when the evil spirit from God was upon Saul, that David took an harp, and played with his hand: so Saul was refreshed, and was well, and the evil spirit departed from him.
>
> —1 Samuel 16:23

The primitive hand-held harp of David's time was played either by strumming with your fingers or with a pick (*plectrum*) when you wanted a harder, louder sound. Again, church musicians take note: Many in our congregation come to worship oppressed by Satan, as well as the world. They need someone who through music can help lift this oppression and fill them once again with joy. This is not entertainment time; it is soul-healing time. This is another reason to question the use of loud, raucous rock music in the sanctuary.

And he [Solomon] spake three thousand proverbs: and his songs [*shir*] were a thousand and five.

—1 Kings 4:32

Recently, scientists studying the human brain at the UCLA medical facility have discovered that whenever a story or written material is sung rather than spoken, it more intensely activates the right hemisphere of the brain, home of what scientists call our "long-term" memory (*LA Times*, Sept. 23, 1998).

It's no accident that tribal cultures for centuries have preserved in song their history and moral lessons to be learned. We know that in the orthodox Jewish synagogues, even today, the Psalms are sung by a cantor (singer) rather than read. Consequently, it shouldn't surprise us to discover that Solomon wrote a large number of songs as well as proverbs. Unfortunately the ancient manuscripts for these songs await discovery.

Solomon was an amazing man. However, unlike his father David, he fell out of love with God and eventually worshipped his own ego, leading Israel into idolatry and civil war. This is a great warning to all of us to always be careful to nurture humility, not pride, through the gifts that God gives us to serve the church.

In 1 Chronicles 15:16–24, we learn that David told the leaders of the Levites to appoint their brothers as singers to sing joyful songs, accompanied by musical instruments (lyres, psalteries, harps, and cymbals). Scripture continues by naming those chosen and the instruments they were to play. Kenaniah, the head Levite, was in charge of the singing. That was his responsibility because he was skillful at it.

These were the first official future temple-appointed musicians. After the construction of the temple by Solomon in 970 b.c. (after David), this team of musicians could swell to four thousand (23:5) for special celebrations and the three annual prescribed feasts.

In Ezra 2:65, after the Babylonian captivity (536 b.c.), we read that besides their 7,337 menservants and maidservants returning to Israel, they also had 200 men and women singers (variation in number recorded in Neh. 7:67). This was when the second temple was built. This temple, although less grand than the temple of Solomon, was still an imposing set of buildings with a large staff of priests and musicians.

Rejoice in the LORD, O ye righteous: for praise is comely for the upright. Praise the LORD with harp [lyres]: sing unto him with the psaltery and an instrument of ten strings. Sing unto him a new song [shir]; play skilfully with a loud noise.

—Psalm 33:1–3

Contemporary rock musicians who want to bring their watered-down pagan music into the church often refer to this passage and others regarding "shouting" for joy as an excuse for assaulting our ears with high-decibel musical madness. There is no correlation. Temple performances, first of all, were outdoors, in the courtyard of the Gentiles or one of the other courtyards. Second, there was no amplification. Third, there were no ear-splitting instrumental accompaniment to this joyful shout.

Let them praise his name in the dance: let them sing praises unto him with the timbrel and harp. For the LORD taketh pleasure in his people: he will beautify the meek with salvation. Let the saints be joyful in glory: let them sing aloud upon their beds [while standing or resting—to be joyful at all times because of God's forgiveness and mercy].

—Psalm 149:3–5

Why should we praise Him even with *dancing?* Because He takes pleasure in us. What a great assurance! Occasionally, we attend a messianic Jewish congregational worship service in our area. Preceding the actual service there are twenty to thirty minutes of sanctified, joyful dancing in the front of the sanctuary for those who wish to celebrate God's mercy, love, and forgiveness. The dancing is dignified and worshipful, and the music is neither loud nor overly syncopated or repetitive. The experience is a joyful one.

And Elijah said unto the prophets of Baal, Choose you one bullock for yourselves, and dress it first; for ye are many; and call on the name of your gods, but put no fire under. And they took the bullock which was given them, and they dressed it, and called on the name of Baal from morning even until noon, saying, O Baal, hear us. But there was no voice, nor any that answered. And they leaped upon the altar which was made.

—1 Kings 18:25–26

Josephus, the Jewish-Roman historian, tells us in his classic *History of the Jews* that these types of pagan rituals were not unaccompanied. They were and still are most distinguished by loud, percussive drumming, repetitive chanting, and sensual syncopation. Obviously, their exertions were to no avail, as are many of the loud, contemporary, sensual, and syncopated songs used today in modern Christian worship. Just as in Elijah's day, this type of worship does not work and God is not amused.

> Take thou away from me the noise of thy songs [*shir*]; for I will not hear the melody of thy viols. [See also Ezek. 26:13.]
>
> —Amos 5:23

God hates meaningless ritual and façade. He wants sincerity, honesty, a heart broken by sin, and true worship, *not a performance glorifying the performer or "entertaining" the congregation.* All music in a worship service should be performed "as unto God," not man.

Singers and musicians must *constantly* be reminded that their sole reason for being there is to (1) glorify God through music and song and (2) unite and spiritually inspire the congregation. Musicians in church must constantly search their hearts for any sign of pride, sensuality, desire to "entertain," or self-aggrandizement. They are to perform with humble, sin-convicted hearts, as though they were singing to our Savior, Jesus Christ *alone*.

No-no's should include: (1) extremely loud, heavily syncopated, overly repetitive music, inappropriate costumes, jewelry, clothes, makeup, (2) lyrics that are scripturally unsound or disrespectful to the Creator of the universe, (3) body language that is sensual or inappropriate to a sanctified setting, (4) distracting lighting or special effects, (5) the encouragement of congregational clapping after the song—*musicians must be constantly reminded that Jesus Christ is the star, not themselves*—and (6) the display or verbal announcements concerning the musicians' CDs, videos, and coming concerts *during the worship service.*

Remember that Christ cleansed the temple not once but twice in His short ministry because of the commerce that was taking place in God's house. If it is a concert, not a worship service, the rules are less stringent than those listed above. However, Christian concerts *must always* put the glorification of our Lord and Savior Jesus Christ *first*, and the importance of delivering a clear and concise message of salvation in music and song. Failure to abide by those two guidelines in a "Christian" concert is a dangerous misrepresentation of the Gospel and Jesus Christ Himself.

How interesting that the last Old Testament scripture dealing with music in a religious service should be a warning about insincere worship. How prophetic in light of the carnal pleasure palaces many of our churches have become, with the headliner to attract the congregation often being a Christian music superstar rather than the Holy Spirit and Jesus Christ Himself.

> But when ye pray, use not *vain repetitions*, as the heathen do: for they think that they shall be heard for their *much speaking. Be not ye therefore like unto them*: for your Father knoweth what things ye have need of, before ye ask him.
>
> —Matthew 6:7–8

When Elijah was taunting the priests of Baal on Mount Carmel in a showdown between their pagan god and the God who was the Creator of the universe, Yahweh, Elijah taunted them because they had been dancing, singing, and chanting to loud, repetitive music for hours *and nothing happened*.

We do not need to "entertain" our God, or appease Him as if He were some sort of spiritual force that could be manipulated through ritual. In this passage, Christ warns us not use these techniques when reaching out in prayer to Him. The pagan cults of His day generally danced, sang, and were accompanied by repetitive, syncopated, percussive loud drumming. They tended to repeat over and over the name of their god, or their request, or both, as if God were hard of hearing. If we correctly interpret that when we come to worship God searches our hearts not our rituals, we will remain solidly on the right path. *Too much music in today's church services sounds more like the babbling of the heathen than sanctified sound.*

> And when Jesus came into the ruler's house, and saw the minstrels and the people making a noise.
>
> —Matthew 9:23

Wealthy individuals hired professional mourners to weep and wail, as well as musicians to play appropriately mournful music upon the death of a member of the family (Jer. 48:36; Amos 5:16). According to the Talmud (Misnayot, chap. 4), even the poorest Israelite usually found the money to hire at least two flutes and a professional wailing woman (Jer. 9:17). The maximum number of accompanying musicians was limited to ten by *Roman* law. One wonders if the Romans had to cap the size of the funeral bands to be able to sleep later in the mornings after a night of debauchery.

> And when they had sung an hymn, they went out into the mount of Olives.
>
> —Matthew 26:30

This scripture describes the completion of the Last Supper and the end of the last lengthy message Christ delivered to His disciples, a powerful message (John 13–17) called the *Upper Room Discourse*. This was ritually correct from the Jewish standpoint. At the end of a typical Passover meal (*seder*), after drinking the third cup of wine, Psalms 115–118 are sung. Then after drinking the fourth cup (which Christ did not—saving it for His return) Psalm 136 is sung, followed by two short closing prayers (Mark 14:26).

There is no indication of musical accompaniment, nor was it traditional in the Jewish celebration of Passover. How sad that today we hear and sing so little a cappella music in our churches. The early Christian church (A.D. 33–320) seldom used accompaniment to the singing of simple hymns and psalms. *There is always the danger of secularizing the music when introducing accompanying instruments, special effects, and voices.*

We are to strip off all of our ego-inflating worldliness when we come before the throne of the living God. How can we do that when we are hearing or singing in a most worldly and carnal, watered-down, or vague confessions of faith and sinfulness? No wonder God waves us off in disgust.

Do not be deceived because the church is large and packed with people. If they are not humbled by the service and made to feel the innate sinfulness of their human nature without the indwelling of the living God through the power of the Holy Spirit, then they have missed the point of worship.

> And be not drunk with wine, wherein is excess; but be filled with the Spirit; Speaking to yourselves in psalms and hymns and spiritual songs, sing-

ing and making melody in your heart *to the Lord*; Giving thanks always for
all things unto God and the Father in the name of our Lord Jesus Christ.

—Ephesians 5:18–20

Music is a *vital part* of interpersonal communications and relationships. (1)
Psalms are the songs of the Bible set to music. (2) Hymns are scriptural songs,
lyrics taken from the Bible, like Hannah's "Magnificat" and the hymns found
in Luke 1 and 2. (3) Spiritual songs are songs *about God and/or scripture* related to issues of faith and life, but not necessarily scripture itself. *All songs
sung or played in a religious service should fall into one of the above three categories.* Silly, simple-minded, contemporary, repetitious, and vacuous songs like
"Jesus Is My Buddy" are offensive to God and those worshipping who are
truly indwelt by the Holy Spirit.

> Let the word of Christ dwell in you richly in all wisdom; teaching and ad-
> monishing one another in [1] *psalms and* [2] *hymns and* [3] *spiritual songs,*
> singing with grace in your hearts to the Lord. And whatsoever ye do in
> word or deed, do all in the name of the Lord Jesus, giving thanks to God
> and the Father by him.
>
> —Colossians 3:16–17

We are to teach *Christ's words and admonitions* to each other through the medium of music. Besides the authenticity and scriptural soundness of the lyrics, the *spiritual maturity and sincerity of the performers is of vital importance.*

> For the Lord himself shall descend from heaven with a shout, with the
> voice of the archangel, and with the *trump of God:* and the dead in Christ
> shall rise first: Then we which are alive and remain shall be caught up to-
> gether with them in the clouds, to meet the Lord in the air: and so shall we
> ever be with the Lord. Wherefore comfort one another with these words.
>
> —1 Thessalonians 4:16–18

There are three types of trumpets used in the Bible:

1. The "trump" of God—as mentioned above and also in Exodus 20, the

same sound God made when appearing to the children of Israel on Mt. Sinai. Here God's trumpet is announcing the glorious event and great mystery—the Rapture of the saints, the bride of Christ.

2. The signal trumpets used by the children of Israel when wandering the desert and, later, to announce special events at the temple in Jerusalem as well as signal blasts for warfare and warnings of coming attacks. These trumpets were either the primitive *shofar* or ram's horn or, later, the ceremonial silver trumpets used in the temple (which have been re-made by the Temple Institute in Jerusalem in preparation for the much longed-for reconstruction of the Jewish temple on the Temple Mount. How that will occur under the current political climate is known only to God, who not only has announced that it will happen [through His prophets], but says, "is there anything too hard for me?" [Isa. 43:12]).

3. The prophetic trumpets announcing God's coming judgment on an unrepentant earth during the final seven years prior to Christ's return—a period the Bible calls the Tribulation. There are seven of these trumpet announcements, beginning in chapter eight of the Book of Revelation through chapter eleven. We are not sure if these trumpets are actually heard on earth, or are just signals of coming judgment announced in Heaven. Angels play these trumpets. Each one announces an increasingly dramatic judgment on sinful mankind.

And when he [Jesus] had taken the book, the four beasts and four and twenty elders fell down before the Lamb, having every one of them harps, and golden vials full of odours, which are the prayers of saints. And they sung a *new song*, saying, Thou art worthy to take the book, and to open the seals thereof: for thou wast slain, and hast redeemed us to God by thy blood out of every kindred, and tongue, and people, and nation; 10 And hast made us unto our God kings and priests: and we [the saints—the church] shall reign on the earth.

—Revelation 5:8–10

This biblical passage portrays one of the most dramatic and important events in the Bible: the repurchasing by the shed blood of our Savior Jesus Christ of the planet earth from Satan, who tricked Adam and Eve into turning it over to him. Naturally there is music; naturally there is a "new" song. Can you imagine the sound of all these voices lifted in praise to the Lord?

> And I heard a voice from heaven, as the voice of many waters, and as the voice of a great thunder: and I heard the voice of harpers harping with their harps: And they sung as it were a *new song* before the throne, and before the four beasts, and the elders: and no man could learn that song but the hundred and forty and four thousand, which were redeemed from the earth.
>
> —Revelation 14:2–3

Well, we now know there's going to be a lot of singing in Heaven and many new songs. This is the second "new song" sung in Heaven. This special group of selected Jewish evangelists play a key role in witnessing during the Tribulation era that are supernaturally protected by the Lord Himself.

Songs

Although we have noted biblical songs in many of the scriptural passages above, it is important to point out in a separate category that songs are consistently used throughout the Bible to celebrate some sort of spiritual gift, victory, or realization. Of course, all of the psalms were written to be sung and, in fact, all of them are sung in an Orthodox Jewish congregation between the Feast of Trumpets (Rosh Hashana) and Yom Kippur in the fall.

In Exodus 15:1–5, Miriam, Moses' sister, sang (written by Moses?) a victory song after the safe passage of the fleeing Jews through the Red Sea and the destruction of pursuing Pharaoh's armies to thank God for the deliverance of His people.

In 2 Samuel 1:18–19, and 3:33, David wrote a song in mourning the death of Saul and Jonathan and another for the death of Abner.

Jeremiah wrote his Lamentations as a dirge following the destruction of Jerusalem by the Babylonian armies in 586 b.c. In 2 Chronicles 35:25, we read another dirge he wrote upon the death of Josiah, king of Judah.

In Judges 5:1–3, Deborah and Barak made a triumphant hymn after the defeat of Sisera.

Both portions of the Song of Solomon and Psalm 45 were written by

King Solomon to be sung, mainly celebrating weddings as well as other songs that contain many allegorical passages.

In 1 Samuel 2:1–2 we read of Hannah's triumphant song for the birth of Samuel.

In Isaiah 38:10–11, good King Hezekiah of Judah returned the thanks to God for the many blessings he had received in song.

In Luke 1:46, 68, and 2:29–30 the songs of the Virgin Mary, Zacharias, the father of John the Baptists, and old Simeon are of the same nature. They are thanksgivings to God for blessings received from him.

And of course the many songs found in the book of Revelation—all an outpouring of joy to our Savior Jesus Christ and His swift move to destroy evil and return to earth and restore it.

Summary

In closing this chapter, I am reminded of a very important and appropriate quote from the pen of C. S. Lewis, one of our greatest Christian apologists and authors:

> We must beware of the naïve idea that our music can please God as it would please a cultivated human hearer. That is like thinking, under the old law, that He really needed the blood of bulls and goats. To which an answer came, "Mine are the cattle upon a thousand hills," and "if I am hungry, I will not tell thee." If God (in that sense) wanted music, He would not tell *us*. For all our offerings, whether of music or martyrdom, are like the intrinsically worthless present of a child, which a father values indeed, *but values it only for the intention.*
>
> —*Christian Reflection*, pp. 98–99

Regarding the contemporary attack on the traditional hymns and songs of the church, many that have been around for three hundred years or longer, I am reminded of another appropriate quote from the pen of C. S. Lewis:

> When I first began attending church services after becoming a Christian I disliked very much many of their hymns, which I considered to be fifth-rate poems set to sixth-rate music. But as I went on I saw the great merit

of it. It came up against different people of quite different outlooks and different education, and then gradually *my conceit just began peeling off.* I realized that the hymns (which were just sixth-rate music) were, nevertheless, being sung with devotion and benefit by an old saint in elastic-side boots in the opposite pew, and then you realize that you aren't fit to clean those boots. It gets you out of your solitary conceit. *It is not for me to lay down laws, as I am only a layman, and I don't know much.*
—God in the Dock, C. S. Lewis, pp. 61–62

What an example of true Christian humility and piety from the pen of one of the greatest Christian apologists to ever live. How I pray today's church musicians would seek spiritual humility instead of worldly pride. Do they honestly believe that the carnal, simple-minded music (often with occult overtones) that they are championing as spiritually correct for a worship service is okay to put before the throne of God? I don't think so.

I truly believe they are using Jesus and the contemporary Laodicean church movement to sell their third-rate songs, lyrics, and performances to a congregation no longer under the conviction of sin but instead are seeking entertainment rather than edification. No wonder Christ stands and knocks at the door of His own church, asking to come [back] in (Rev. 3). God has been dethroned for sensual self-worship. We have sold our spiritual heritage for a cold cup of porridge; however, it is not too late to repent if you are part of this Christian rock movement or support it in any way. First John 1:9 applies to all: if we confess and turn from our sin, He is quick to forgive and forget. Why not do it now? Let go of this demonic intrusion into Christian worship. Rebuke it and turn from it and God will heal the mind and the soul and will lift coming judgment. To ignore this warning is to place self, family, and church in spiritual jeopardy. Christ is coming for a pure bride, clothed in white. He is *not* coming for an artificially stimulated congregation of paganized worshippers.

The Afro-American (Black) Church

African Americans have contributed significantly to sanctified, worshipful music. Do not confuse what I say in this book with an attack on the music of the black church. In fact, most black churches are *a great deal more sensitive* to what is appropriate and what is not appropriate regarding music and worship. They are much more careful about rhythms, volume, lyric content, and the spiritual attitude of the singers and musicians than most "white" churches today.

Spirituals (Pre-Civil War). Negro spirituals contain some of the richest, most honest religious music of early America. "Goin' Home," an early popular Negro spiritual, was used by Anton Dvörak, Romanian composer visiting the United States at the turn of the century, as the primary theme of his popular *New World Symphony*. Spirituals were sung, for the most part, unaccompanied. Soloists were sometimes featured, but not always. The emphasis on the lyrics was on the promise of a better life in Heaven.

Early Gospel (1865–1920s). Early gospel sprang up in the small storefront churches in New Orleans and wherever else there was a sizeable black population. The emphasis was now on the importance of salvation: being saved. Guitar, and sometimes organ or piano or harmonica, often accompanied them. The tambourine was often used to add a little spice to the more rhythmic tunes.

Middle Gospel (1920s–1960s). A former black blues-singer going by the stage name of "Tampa Red" found the Lord in one of these small storefront churches while still a young man. He abandoned his career as a blues singer (unlike today, musicians in those days knew they could not walk both sides of the musical street—sacred and secular—successfully) and began traveling from church to church, introducing a more sophisticated but still sanctified form of gospel music. This man's name was *Thomas A. Dorsey.*

Probably his most popular gospel song was "Precious Lord," written shortly after receiving notice from home that his wife had died suddenly. There is a wonderful VHS video out titled *Say Amen Somebody!* that documents his life and many of the leading gospel singers and musicians of the time. Ray Charles, Etta James, Aretha Franklin, Stevie Wonder, and many others who became pop stars began in gospel music.

Late Gospel (1960s—present). Moving on to more modern productions and tune-types without compromising their integrity, this period spawned some of the most influential contemporary Christian musical artists of all time, including Andre Crouch, Al Greene, The Waymans, and many others.

A Lesson to Be Learned

For the most part, the black church has more successfully introduced and used modern musical styles and recording techniques *without sacrificing their spiritual integrity.* Drums have been used in the churches, but are seldom too loud. The same is true for the organ and the electric bass. The guitar, if used at all, is usually tastefully done. *Pagan, highly syncopated rhythms are avoided.*

The black church seems to know that there is a fine line between acceptable and unacceptable music for worship. Their pastors, music directors, and congregations seem to be more aware of the power and the dangers of music used in a careless manner. I believe there is a lesson to be learned out all this. If only these large, loud, pride-filled spiritual arenas of today were listening.

The Beginning of
the Jesus-Rock Movement

The Hook

The incredible power of rock music and its universal appeal to young people began to seep into church music in the late 1960s and early '70s. Was it the "devil's music," as some claimed, or was it possible to use this new universally popular musical style to attract people to church, particularly young people? Was it the "hook" that would help stop the decline in church attendance, particularly among young adults?

Jesus Movement

An interesting development in the "hippie" movement of the '60s–'80s was the birth of what came to be known as the *Jesus Movement*. Burned-out hippies, with lives shattered by illicit sex, drugs, alcohol, and a voluntary descent into hell through hallucinogenic drugs, began turning to Christ for salvation and for help. Many had tried everything else and they had nothing to lose. Buddha didn't do it; Mohammed didn't do it; Krishna didn't do it . . . maybe Jesus Christ was the answer.

In Costa Mesa, California, a young pastor by the name of Chuck Smith, disenchanted with the tunnel vision and legalism of mainline denominations began his own independent ministry. His area was a Mecca for surfers, hippies, and those desperately looking for some way out of the self-created hell of hippiedom. Chuck Smith invited them to come to church "just as they were," with cut-offs, sandals, beads, long hair, and hollowed eyes. He even allowed them to keep their style of music, with new lyrics of course, lyrics that honored Christ, the Bible, salvation, etc.

This new type of practicing Christianity and worship spread like wildfire, within and without the United States. Soon, recording studios were crowded with young Christian musicians recording their new songs. Christian record labels and publishing companies sprang up, along with independent FM stations to broadcast the music.

Pioneers in this field included *Al Greene*, a popular black rhythm 'n blues singer who decided to concentrate on contemporary Christian music, and *Andre Crouch*, a powerful singer-songwriter with an excellent ensemble who could have gone on to make zillions of dollars in the wider commercial world of rock, but chose to stay with CCM (contemporary Christian music).

Other pioneers included *Bill Gaither*, who combined the traditional southern gospel style with the new music, *Amy Grant*, *Ralph Carmichael*, and many others. *Pat Boone*, already a widely known pop singer, *Johnny Cash*, and even *Elvis Presley* himself recorded Christian LPs for this rapidly growing market.

> **Art in its final degeneration exists only to shock.**
>
> —George Orwell

The Bible is full of expositions on sacred rock music. Music was an integral part of ancient cultures. We can go back to the Exodus, and we are told in 1 Corinthians 10:11 that these examples are written in scripture as guidelines for *us today*. The first powerful rock concert recorded in the Bible was the one that the children of Israel participated in while Moses was up on Mt. Sinai receiving the Word of God in the form of the Ten Commandments and the dimensions and meanings in the construction of the tabernacle.

> The technical differences between "serious" (modern classical) music, jazz, rock or any other form of modern music was less important than the underlying factor that *they're philosophical basis was more or less one and the same: hedonism and anarchy.*
>
> —David Tame, *The Secret Power of Music*, p. 103

Probably the words being sung were okay, but the music was Egyptian, occultic, loud, repetitious, and trance-inducing. Moses and Joshua heard the celebration from afar (Exod. 32:5). Joshua thought it sounded like "the noise of war in the camp" (Exod. 32:17). Were they rewarded for the musical celebration? Hardly. Swift and severe judgment followed (Exod. 32:18–end).

Sloppy Agape
If people knew what this stuff [rock music] was about, we'd probably all get arrested.

—Bob Dylan, 1966 interview, *Rolling Stone*

Later in scripture we find in Leviticus 10:1–2 that the sons of Aaron (Levitical priests serving in the tabernacle) were swiftly punished for mixing *the sacred and the profane.*

Moral Corruption
There's gonorrhea, syphilis, AIDS, rabies, NSU, venereal warts and herpes. Man, you'd simply be amazed at the number of times one has to go to the VD clinic; it's almost a regular stop for some groups on the way to or from a gig . . . the wallowing through the muck and mire of sleaze is all part of the rock and roll lifestyle.

—*Cream,* quote from a leading rock star of the '70s, October 1981, p. 32

In the Book of Numbers Balaak, king of the Edomites, hired Balaam, a local prophet-priest (of unscriptural practices), to put a curse on the children of Israel as they migrated through the land of the Edomites on the way to the Promised Land. Failing each time in being able to put a curse on Israel, Balaam finally confessed that the only way to weaken Israel would be to send the most seductive women (along with their seductive native dances) to the young Israeli men and soon they would intermarry and eventually embrace false gods. *Idolatry was a major problem for Israel from that moment* (around 1200 b.c.) until the *end of the Babylonian captivity* (around 536 b.c.). Certainly pagan music was part of these sensual practices.

David and the Ark (1 Chronicles 13,15)
God says what He means and means what He says in Scripture. In moving the Ark of the Covenant from Shiloh to Jerusalem, King David got careless and let a non-Levite carry the Ark and he himself danced almost naked in

front of it. As a result, when the Ark tipped, Uzza died as a result of touching it; you see, he and David and the rest were *all guilty of deliberate disobedience.* David realizes his mistake and later says that as God prescribed, *only Levites* were allowed to carry or move the Ark.

Spiritual Deception

More than any other form of the misuse of sound, it is rock with which we must deal today. . . . It is a global phenomenon; a pounding destructive beat which is heard from America and Western Europe to Africa and Asia. Its effect upon the soul is to make nigh-impossible the true inner silence and peace necessary for the contemplation of eternal verities. . . . How *necessary* is it in this age *for some to have the courage to be the ones who are "different"; and to separate themselves out from the pack* who long ago sold their lives and personalities to this sound. . . . I adamantly believe that *rock in all its forms* is a critical problem which our civilization *must* get to grips . . . if it wishes long to survive.

—David Tame, *The Secret Power of Music,* p. 204

In the dramatic and prophetic outline of end-time events just preceding His return in what Bible scholars call the Olivet Discourse (Matt. 24–25; Mark 13; Luke 21) Christ warns that the single most predominant sign of the end times would be *spiritual deception.* As we know from Ezekiel 28 and Isaiah 13, Satan was at one time in charge of worship and understood well the power of music. Paul says in 2 Corinthians 11:13–15 that Satan and his fallen angels can transform themselves into "angels of light," meaning false teachers, singers, and musicians within the body of Christ. Second Thessalonians 2 echoes the tremendous and powerful deception that will take place *within* as well as without the Body of Christ.

Spiritual Babylon

Take thou away from me the noise of thy songs; for I will *not* hear the melody of thy viols.

—Amos 5:23

Music was an important part of ceremonies and worship in ancient Babylon under the Nebuchadnezzar (Dan. 3:5). End-time Babylon is full of harpists, musicians, pipers, and trumpeters (Rev. 18:22). We are told to *come out* of that kind of environment, not bring it into the church. Throughout history, there have only been two choices: either we take the church out into sinful society or allow sinful society into the church. Compromise may be the heart of politics, but it is deadly dangerous in the spiritual realm. *There can be no compromise with God's Word or His practices without bringing judgment.*

"Begone, I Never Knew You"

Rock 'n Roll is one of the most lucrative industries in the world, with $15 billion in annual sales. In the U.S.A., record sales are larger than that of the *combined* grosses of motion pictures, television, professional sports and Broadway theater.

—*Hell's Bells* video by David Holmberg, 2001

One of the most frightening passages in the Bible for me is found in Matthew 7, toward the end of the Sermon on the Mount. Christ warns that there will be many that will some day stand before Him for judgment and will claim that they preached in His name, healed in His name and I'm sure "sang" and "played music" in His name. Christ's answer is chilling: *"Begone, I never knew you."* How can contemporary pastors today play fast and loose with God's Word, God's guidelines for worship, and God's strict regulations concerning the church?

The Great Harlot

Appropriate Christian Music: does it stir the flesh to "boogie," or the spirit to "Praise the Lord? It cannot be both!

—radio interview, JW , 2003

Marked for destruction, the great spiritual harlot (found in Revelation 12–13 and destroyed in Revelation 17) is called a "harlot" because she openly mixes *the sacred with the profane.* Music can and has become part of this unholy mixture. For almost two thousand years in the Christian church and another almost two thousand years of Judaism preceding Christ, very specific guidelines were given for worship. Suddenly these guidelines are being ignored and the mixture of the sacred and the profane is openly boasted of. How can this be? Is there no fear of the living God?

Walk the Talk

Rock contains harmonic dissonance and melodic discord while it accents rhythm with a big beat. In fact, the anapestic beat (two short beats, a long beat, than a pause) used by many rock musicians actually is *the exact opposite of our heart and arterial rhythms*, thereby causing an *immediate loss of body strength.*"

—Dr. David Nobel, *"Music's Surprising Power to Heal,"*
August 1992, *Reader's Digest*

Another medical doctor and leading researcher in the field of music, Dr. Diamond, confirms Dr. Nobel's remarks and adds that the stopped anapestic rhythm (of rock music) *"heightens stress and anger, reduces output, increases hyperactivity, and weakens muscle strength"* (Ibid.).

Paul said in 2 Timothy 3:5 that we are living in a time when we will talk more and more about Jesus but remain the same in our carnal nature. That's why our Lord Jesus Christ told us to look for the "fruits" of the ministry. Today the divorce rate, child and wife abuse rate, and other moral corrupting behaviors are almost as high within the church as without. Babylon has so closely counterfeited worship that it is unsafe to judge worship by *our feelings alone.* Everything must line up with Scripture—Scripture in context, not out of context—or *it does not belong.* This includes the guidelines for music.

Scripture-Twisting

Larry Norman, frequently dubbed "the father of Christian rock," makes the statement that rock 'n roll music *"originated in the Church hundreds of years ago, and that the devil stole it!"* His battle cry is to *"take rock music back for Jesus' sake!"*

—*www.rapidnet.com/~jbeard/bdm/Psychology/rockm/satanic.htm*

Defenders of Christian rock point out the Bible commands us to "sing a new song unto the Lord" (Ps. 40:3). Does that mean we stop singing the sanctified hymns and praise songs of the past? *I don't think so!* What does the Bible mean about singing a "new" song? In Revelation 15:3 we see that this *new* song is *none other than the 3,500-year-old song from Exodus, the song of Moses and the Lamb.*

Sanctuary

> Rock music calls to all the baser instincts of man—riots, rebellion, sexual sensuality, sexual gratification, self-glorification. Rock music was designed to excite and stimulate the flesh.
>
> —Wayman Zeldon, *www.bibletruths.org/rock_music*

When one wishes to escape the hustle and bustle of the modern world—its aggressive, narcissistic self-centeredness; its relentless pumping of loud music and obnoxious images into our consciousness—where do you go? There are only two places left: the quietness of nature and the church. Sadly, the church is quickly disappearing as a sanctuary, as a holy place where one can go and hear the "whisper" of God through prayer, Bible study, and meditation.

It's a great blessing to leave a worship service feeling calm, loving, and spiritually uplifted. It is quite another to feel agitated, vexed, anxious, embarrassed, and resentful after being subject to almost constant rock music.

Throughout the history of the Christian church, believers have always had one of two choices to make: either (1) take the church out into corrupt, sinful society, or (2) invite corrupt sinful practices of society into the church in the hope of winning converts. Scripture endorses only one: the church must go out *without compromise to fulfill the Word of God.*

For three hundred years, from the time of the resurrection of Jesus Christ (A.D. 32), the church was small, persecuted, and centered on the Word of God and the guidance of the Holy Spirit. When the church became a state religion throughout the Roman Empire under the edict of Emperor Constantine (A.D. 312) the church *compromised* and allowed many ancient pagan customs, many traceable to ancient Babylon, into the church. The church grew in size *but diminished in spiritual power.*

Recent History

In the early 1950s, Cleveland disco jockey Allan Freed coined the term "rock 'n roll" which, up until this time had been called "rhythm 'n blues," and had been a popular style of dance music in the black community. The term itself, "rock 'n roll," describes sexual activity, always a close associate of the music.

The extreme volume, heavy backbeat of the drums, repetitive phrases, and syncopated rhythm patterns all combined to create a sensory overload and triggered the "fight-or-flight" response. For the first time in our culture, music was being used as a drug . . . yet few understood what was happening.

The Christian church resisted the desire to bring the music into the church until the 1970s when the success of new ministries that allowed this kind of music (with Christian lyrics) into the sanctuary during the worship service rubbed off on more traditional churches who were losing members. Soon there was a whole new category of commercial music in the United States: "Christian" rock/pop, etc. The records and CDs sold by early pioneers like the Maranatha Publishing Co, Bill Gaither, the Imperials, Dallas Holmes, Randy Stonehill, Keith Greene, and others, became the hottest selling items in Christian bookstores across America, eventually representing $2–3 billion annually of a $12–15 billion a year record industry.

Today, every type of pop/rock music that is commercially available is also available in a more "sanitized" version in Christian music. Parents breathe a sigh of relief, because the believe (erroneously) that a few "amens" and "Jesus'" thrown in occasionally somehow sanctifies a musical style built on the slogan, "sex, drugs and rock 'n roll." As we've already seen in this report, this music is not new; in fact it represents some of the oldest music in the world: the occultic, orgiastic, pagan, blatantly sexual music of ancient Babylon, Egypt, Greece, and Rome and their sensual religious cults.

Sensory Overload

An estimated 60% of all the Rock and Roll stars that are inducted into the Rock 'n Roll Hall of Fame in Cleveland, Ohio have significant hearing loss.

—*www.evangelicaloutreach.org/mus_02/htm*

The human ear is a delicate mechanism. It does not take much overloading to begin the deterioration process. Anything over 80 decibels is potentially dangerous. The average rock festival volume is around 90 to 100 decibels, depending on where you sit.

Yet, "modern" pastors like Rick Warren boast that their "Christian" music is very loud and rock/pop based. Isn't it interesting that the church used to be known for peace and quiet, but today you could actually damage your hearing by attending some of these loud Christian-rock led services.

Dr. Bernard Sherman in his recent book, *Losing Your Ears to Music* esti-
mates that there are twelve million rock fans in the USA with "tinnitus," a
constant and persistent ringing in the ears.

—*www.edu-cyberpg.com/music*

As we've already studied, the constant sharp pounding of the rock drummer
on the backbeats (beats 2 and 4) triggers the survival mechanism we all have
called the "fight-or-flight" response. The sudden rush of adrenaline into the
bloodstream gives us a "rush" and increases aggression. Sadly, the modern
church mistakes this as a symbol of the presence of the Holy Spirit. Nothing
could be further from the truth.

I'm a single officer alone with my car and you can hear this guy's car for
blocks. He still hasn't turned anything down yet. It's a real low, bassy thing
and you could feel it. If he'd had a cup of water on his dashboard it would
look like Jurassic Park. I finally got him to turn it off by making gestures.
I'm in shock that this guy can even hear me, then he reaches up behind his
ears and puts in his hearing aid. . . . *He is 22 years old and is almost totally
deaf in his right ear.* He's really cooperative. I asked him when he lost his
hearing and he said, "Oh, about a year ago—the doctors said the music
was too loud." I asked him why he did it, and he just said, "'Cause, man,
it's the thing to do!"

—*San Diego Union Tribune*, October 18, 2001, Music Scene, p. 9

Ironically, some of the loudest rock music today is in the church or at major
evangelical outreaches like Billy Graham's Crusades and Greg Laurie's Harvest Crusades. Three years ago we took one of our sons and grandsons to the
San Diego Harvest Crusade. I had to warn everyone to put their fingers in
their ears during some of the musical presentation or *risk serious and permanent hearing loss.* Apparently it's not even safe to send your kids to a Christian
crusade anymore.

In another instance, a group from my Bible class went to a Sandi Patti
concert at a major church in San Diego. The very first part of the concert was
wonderful (she repeated some of her timeless hits), but very quickly it dis-
solved into a Christian rock gospel concert and she and a black male singer
were screaming and shouting so loud we had to leave, terribly disappointed.

Audiologist Kathleen Bulley tests and evaluates hearing at *Scripps Hospital in LaJolla*. She has noticed an increase in young adults coming forward with *hearing loss*. . . . Bulley says there is a very *real danger* to *listening to loud music*. . . . It usually starts out in the high-frequency range—like how your ears feel stuffed after a *loud concert*. . . . According to OSHA (governmental) guidelines 90 decibels for *eight hours* can cause *permanent hearing loss*. At 100 dB's—two hours; at 105—one hour. At 180 dB people start to feel like *they're coming apart*.

—*San Diego Union Tribune*, October 18, 2001, Music Scene, p. 9

Noise pollution is a very dangerous problem in our society and, unfortunately, the new "seeker-sensitive" churches that not only allow but promote this kind of music are apparently unknowingly endangering the hearing of their congregations—even though there is ample scientific evidence warning us about volume in music and its dangers.

Resist the Devil and He Will Flee From You (James 4:7)

Since jazz and the blues were the parents of rock and roll, this also means that there exists a direct line of descent from the voodoo ceremonies of Africa, through jazz, to rock and roll and all the other forms of rock music today.

—David Thane, *The Secret Power of Music*, p. 103

I strongly urge every Christian who attends church regularly to resist the efforts to bring Christian rock music into the sanctuary during worship. Please point out the dangers as illuminated by the material in this book, my previous two books *All That Jazz: A History of Afro-American Music* and *Crisis in Christian Music*, all available through *amazon.com* on the Internet. In addition, check out the Internet yourself. Through a search engine like Google type in "rock music in the church." You will get a ton of material from a wide range of sources all sincerely pointing out the dangers of this music.

Big Business

Rock music specifically is, *a negative influence on both the physical body and moral nature of man.*

—David Thane, *The Secret Power of Music*, p. 136

Christian rock/pop music is one of the fastest growing parts of today's $12 billion annual payroll. So many parents are under the illusion that if it is packaged and sold through a Christian bookstore, it must be okay. In most instances, it's not. Even the lyrics have become increasingly corrupted and have moved further and further away from Scripture and the glorification of Jesus Christ, and more and more into the camp of self-indulgent spiritual narcissism.

> It is not just a "phase" that teens go through as some have erroneously thought. The philosophy is that what a person fills his or her mind with at 15 will, *short of an absolute creative miracle by God,* continue to permeate their thinking at 35 and beyond. And when one considers that today's teens listen to an average of *10,500 hours of rock music between the 7th and 12th grades.*
>
> —U.S. News & World Report, October 28, 1985, p. 46

Styles

Today, Christian rock imitates or "mocks" commercial styles and artists, even to the "gangsta" clothes, dress, sullen looks, rebellious and sensual poses for CD covers, etc. *The only difference is an occasional—and I do mean occasional—reference to Jesus Christ and Christianity.* The market is obviously aimed at preteens (eight- to twelve-year-olds) and teenagers (thirteen- to twenty-year-olds), with girls being the primary market.

Stylistically there is (1) mainstream Christian pop, (2) teeny-bopper rock (the youngest kids), (3) heavy metal, (4) gothic, (5) ethnic, (6) hip-hop, (7) rhythm 'n blues, (8) country-rock , (9) rap, and (10) "gangsta rap." Each of these popular styles has its followers among today's teenagers. We now even have Christian "rap" music, a musical style completely devoid of melody, harmony, dynamics, etc. It is a style of "protest" music that goes back to ancient Africa and the tribal riots.

Christian "Evangelism" Through Music

Many of today's popular Christian rock groups state that their primary purpose is *evangelism,* although seldom in their concerts is the plan of salvation given, Scripture read, or an altar call made. The Bible states that music's purpose is primarily for *worship*, not evangelism. *There is not one instance in Scripture where music is used for evangelism.* The Holy Spirit through the Word of God, the Bible, is what brings sinners under conviction, not suggestively clad, overtly loud, brazen, and prideful performances of wealthy and powerful Christian rock stars and groups.

Why do these groups advertise primarily on Christian radio and television and through supportive local churches? Because an estimated 80 percent of their income from record sales comes through Bible bookstores and churches. *It's a big business folks, with bookstores, publishers, record companies, and mega-churches all lining up for their piece of the action* (see www.rapidnet.com/~jbeard/bdm/Psychology/rockm/satanic.htm).

AIDS and Rock Music

Black [Afro-American] researchers were horrified when they interviewed young inner city black males about sex. It was the researcher's introduction to the attitudes that are now cliches in the *hip-hop* videos and *playa* movies; the casual disposal of women as *"hos,"* used [sexually] *without regard to pregnancy, disease or other consequences.*

—*San Diego Union Tribune*, April 4, 2004, Book Section

Mosh Pits

Many commercial rock concerts and even some rock clubs offer what is called a "mosh pit" for "dancers." A mosh pit is an area (usually in front of the stage) where individuals and couples can go and *do anything they like* short of public sex or exposure. Mosh pits often get violent, with individuals hurling their bodies at each other. At commercial concerts, well-trained bouncers surround the mosh pit and stop any activity or individual that gets too far out of line. Here's the surprise: *mosh pits are a common event at most major Christian rock concerts.* Most parents are not aware of this.

Visualization of Pop Music

The power of MTV is enormous. The last time I visited Israel, I had the opportunity to talk to a major executive of an international hotel chain in Jerusalem. He told me that families from all over the world who come to visit Israel and Jerusalem insist on two things: access to CNN and MTV—CNN for the parents, MTV for the kids. MTV now controls a great deal of the pop record industry, dominates the television channels for teenagers (who have the most discretionary income of all), and now they've moved into producing motion pictures.

The programming of MTV is primarily a visualization of popular rock hits. These visualizations are often borderline pornographic, sensual, violent, and degrading to women, and occasionally to children and animals. The major themes, over and over again, are sex, the occult (demons, charms, Satan, etc.), violence, lust, power, anger, gender hatred, adult hatred, hatred for society, hatred for law and order, and drugs. The videos produced by the top Christian rock groups are not much better, just a bit more reserved, with only ambiguous lyrics and motions regarding the most common topics of their commercial big sister. I challenge all adults and particularly parents to spend a few hours watching MTV, realizing that they have a bigger impact on today's youth than any other input or source.

Hooked on the Music

NBC Television's Tom Brokaw now openly associates the cause of much of our teenage social unrest, crime, murders and rape with today's music and entertainment.

—"The Brokaw Report," NBC Television, June 5, 1992

The powerful musical and sometimes visual signals sent by this occult-based music is hard to overcome. The "high" teenagers get from the fight-or-flight rush they get when they listen to loud music with a sharp backbeat is like a drug; teenagers and, today, many adults *cannot live without it. That's one of the primary reasons the rockers of the 1960s and '70s have insisted on bringing their music, their drug, into the church.*

Nyet

The Christian church (evangelical Protestant) in Russia today is more aware of the dangers of Christian rock than we are. Recently Peter Peters and Vasilij Ryzhuk, head of a Russian church conglomerate called the *Unregistered Union of Churches* wrote a letter to major Christian rock stars and their record companies *urging* them not to bring that kind of music to Russia:

Our young people do not attend these concerts or meetings [where contemporary American Christian rock music is performed] because *we have
all committed not to participate in secular entertainment.* Many come with
Bible in hand and rock music. We are *embarrassed by this image of Christianity.* . . . We abhor all Christian rock music coming to our country.

Rock music has nothing in common with ministry or service to God.
We are very, very against Americans bringing to our country this false
image of "ministry" to God. We need spiritual bread—give us true bread,
not false cakes. It is true that rock music attracts people to the church, but
not to godly living.

—*www.behtlministries.com/russian.htm*

Play It and They Will Come

The single most common argument from pastors, worship directors, and
musicians themselves are that *young people will not attend church without rock
music.* There are no studies that I could find that support that claim in any
way. In fact, there are numerous studies that claim just the opposite: teenagers *do not want to go to church and hear "bad" or "amateurish" rock music. They
go to worship as we do with appropriate music.*

In 1995 Dr. Barbara Resch conducted a survey of nearly five hundred
teenagers from across the U.S.A. on the appropriateness of music for the
church. The findings are surprising. The vast majority of teenagers in this
survey agreed on the following. The preferred music and styles were:

1. Choral music, not instrumental
2. Sung by a group of singers rather than a soloist.
3. Characterized by a simple musical texture and understandable text

Musical examples reminiscent of popular styles (rock, jazz, and country)
were *overwhelmingly rejected as church music.*

The study goes on to record that though most of these teenagers liked
rock music and thought it was the right music for some times and places in
their lives, they didn't believe that the church service was that time and place.
Another surprise in the survey was the discovery that the responses were

not significantly different from the teens who attended church regularly and those who did not. In fact, while listening to examples of Christian rock/pop, many responded, "This sounds like my parent's music!"

When asked regarding their feelings on the role of music in worship the most common responses were (in order)

1. Church music should be an expression of religious belief.
2. Church music is part of the presentation of God's Word (the Bible).
3. Church music is a way for people to use their talents to serve God.
4. Church music establishes or changes people's moods.

The final results continue to surprise us. Those surveyed showed a healthy respect for the corporate nature of their worshiping congregations. In other words, they were sensitive the effects of introducing rock music on the older members of the congregation! The summary of this study is stunning:

> Attempts by adults to present an appealing contemporary popular sound were apparently unsuccessful in winning over unchurched students, who measure that sound against cutting-edge pop music and *found it lacking.*
> —*http://worship.lcms.org/insert/churchmusic/91teens.html*

In other words, non-church–going teens would not or could not be seduced into attending church on a regular basis because of the introduction of amateurish, watered-down pop/rock music with quasi-religious lyrics . . . something I have said for many years now.

I have run my own survey in this area and it supports this study and others. So why do pastors keep telling us the kids won't come to church without this kind of music? I don't think that is the primary reason for its unpopular introduction into contemporary Christian worship. I believe it is all part of a vast pattern to secularize the church in an effort to attract more members . . . casual dress, drama sketches, guest musical artists, special lighting, emotion-wrenching testimonies, and ear-splitting music. We have turned worship into a circus, leaving Christ outside to knock on the door and ask to come back in to His own church (Rev. 3—Laodicean Church).

Who's Influencing Who?

Two arguments today about music: (1) the ancients and the traditionalists believe that music affects character and society, and therefore the artist has a duty to be *responsibly moral and constructive, not immoral and destructive.* The other argument (2) is the opinion of the secular humanists, the radical *avant garde:* that music is basically "amoral," that is neutral in its ability to influence positively or negatively.

This point of view is part of the greater foundation of our culture philosophically today. We live in an era of moral relativism, born out of existentialism and socialism along with Darwinism . . . basically, man is only responsible for himself and all his moral points of view are personal, not communal. Under this philosophy a president of the United States could lie under oath concerning his "immoral" behavior in the Oval Office of the White House and *mean it!* No one takes responsibility for their lives; we are all victims of circumstance.

No wonder the Gospel message is such a hard-sell today, for the God of the Bible holds us individually and collectively responsible for our behavior and only through the shed blood of an innocent lamb, the Lamb of God, Jesus Christ, can the blot of sin be erased and judgment spared. How ironic to see people today supposedly within the body of Christ taking the second position regarding their music, their lives, their way of worship, and their watered-down and often insulting presentation of the path of salvation.

Roots

Rock music is a sad, exaggerated imitation of authentic black American rhythm 'n blues. This music, born in the juke joints and honky-tonks of black rural America crossed the color line into the white community in the 1960s. Black Americans understood the roots of this music and forbade its playing in black churches. It was called "the devil's music," and still is—to most Christian Afro-Americans.

Thomas A. Dorsey, the father of modern black gospel, and the author of such wonderful modern praise-songs as *Precious Lord*, was himself a former blues singer by the name of "Tampa Red" before he became saved and turned his musical talents toward serving the Lord.

Imitation

Whenever a foreign culture adopts the characteristics of another culture the foreign culture always exaggerates the artistic styles of the culture they are borrowing from. White Americans took the native rhythm 'n blues of black Americans and distorted its rhythms, increased the volume of the music, and turned the lyrics into songs of rage and rebellion.

To this day, the Afro-American churches, for the most part, have resisted the intrusions of commercial "Christian" rock music into their churches. They see the crass commercialism, distortions, and prideful nature of the music for what it is.

Rock 'n Roll

The first style of rock was called "rock 'n roll." The origin of this title is traced to Bo Diddley, a well-known black rhythm 'n blues artist of the '60s and '70s who coined the term to describe the cheap imitation of black rhythm 'n blues by white cover (imitative) artists.

He told Allen Freed, one of the first rock disc jockeys in Cleveland, Ohio, that this music, "rock 'n roll" suggests the motion of a couple making love. When someone sings, "I want to rock and roll all night," they are talking about more than dancing.

Rebellion

We all know that the '60s and '70s were decades of rebellion. Lapel buttons that read "Question Authority" were popular, along with a communal lifestyle and anything that could be seen as a rejection of traditional American cultural values. Sex became a sport, drugs a religious communal experience (as still are among the Jamaican Rastafarians and certain sects of Hinduism), and the music had to overwhelm the senses and attack all traditional social values.

People stopped "listening" to music in an intellectual and emotionally stimulating (but controlled) way and started "feeling" music instead. The critical nature was set aside as long as the music overwhelmed the senses. For this to happen, the music had to overcome the logical, deductive, and comparative—experience parts of our brain and open us up to non-logical sensory experiences, foreign (until then) to most Western cultures. Music was used to create feelings and not new understandings.

Using music to open up man's mind to hallucinatory experiences is not new. It was and is quite common even today in many cultures. Even in the days of our Lord, this kind of music was common, particularly to the religious cults. Remember that it was Jesus who cautioned His followers not to "babble" (use non-logical repetitions to overcome critical areas of the brain) as the heathen.

Music As a Drug

Music can be used as a drug. Loud, sudden, sharp sounds, such as the backbeat of the rock drummer, tend to activate the "fight-or-flight" response (read my book, *Crisis in Christian Music*, for a more detailed explanation). Early man had to face sudden danger and *loud, repetitive, sharp sounds* were and still are interpreted by our brain as "danger."

When this fight-or-flight response is activated, the brain sends a signal to the adrenal glands, located above the kidneys. Adrenaline is then dumped into the blood stream, giving us a sudden surge of energy and aggression— the power to fight or flight (run).

Repetitive (Chanting)

All cults use some form of repetitive chanting to break down individual consciousness. This is necessary to remove the "logical" part of our normal thinking, otherwise we would see through the charade of occult practices and realize that they are false and dangerous. All forms of overly repetitive chanting or singing of a simple line over and over are dangerous and are contrary to biblical teaching.

Syncopated Rhythms

When I was researching my book *All That Jazz: A History of Afro-American Music*, I discovered that most of the tribal religions of Africa, Latin America, Asia, and Polynesia were demonic in nature and relied on certain rhythms to call up the spirits peculiar to that religion. This discovery was later confirmed by a scholarly book called *Drumming on the Edge of Magic* by Mickey Hart, drummer for the well-known rock group *The Grateful Dead*.

Church Music

Historically, the Christian church has long suspected that the deadly combination of the three musical characteristics given above was not only not scriptural but also contrary to true worship. For centuries the church forbade certain rhythms, restricted the volume of the music, and avoided mindless repetition. Even plainsong, or early Gregorian chant, though melodically repetitious, avoided mindless repetition of the lyrics.

Most sects within Christianity resisted secular music coming into the sanctuary until the 1960s. One of the concerns was the loss of the sense of "holiness" and another was the danger of church music moving from being a tool to promote worship to becoming a form of entertainment.

One of the tragic losses in accepting rock music into the sanctuary and the church service is the loss of "holiness." One feels as if he or she is at a rock concert or some sort of spiritual pep rally. Holiness has been replaced with commercial slickness, light shows, rock bands, and other commercial techniques used to "dazzle" the congregation.

The Role of the Church

Until the mid-twentieth century in America, the role of the church was to take Christ and the church into the world, not bring the world into the church. Most pastors understood that the world and its sensual nature were incompatible with a life of holiness. Churches and pastors were more concerned with following the dictates of God in running a church as outlined in Scripture than in attracting hundreds, even thousands, to their services. Pastors, elders, deacons, and church congregations relied upon the Holy Spirit to attract new believers, not worldly, mass-marketing techniques.

Today a staff meeting at a mega-church looks, feels, and acts more like a corporate boardroom or a Hollywood studio than a spiritual gathering. The Bible, prayer, and reliance on the Holy Spirit for guidance in running the church has been cast away for corporate pep talks, a search for new and "exciting" forms of entertainment, flashy special affects, etc.

Resistance

Christ compares His followers to sheep. We are sheep, but we need a shepherd. The phenomena of mass or group intimidation of a congregation regarding the questioning or protesting of any change in church policy by any-one at any level of church authority is weak or nonexistent.

The doctrine of the Nicolaitians, which Christ said in Revelation 2 that He "hated," has leapt from the Catholic to the non-Catholic denominations. What is this doctrine? It is the doctrine that places church leaders *above* the laity or congregation, meaning they are, if not infallible, at least *not* subject to normal protests and questions of authority. This feeling is so subtle that many churches and parishioners are not aware of it.

Seldom are pastors in churches *ever* approached with anything but ac-colades, unless he or she has blatantly broken the basic rules of morality, and even then it is more to avoid embarrassing the church than rebuking the pas-tor. Strong personalities, who are not afraid to challenge authority in busi-ness and civic environments, are often strangely silent in a religious context.

Most believe that God is closer to the pastor and church leadership than they are. As a result rather, than resisting change when it should be resisted, the people in the congregation remain silent, or stop coming to church, or search out another body of believers.

This is contrary to Scripture. Even a casual reading of the Book of Acts, 1 and 2 Corinthians, Hebrews, Galatians, and 1, 2 and 3 John reveal and ex-pose the fact that not only are we to speak up when we sense the pastor or the church is headed in the wrong direction, *we are spiritually obligated to do so.*

Tradition

Another sad by-product of allowing a commercial, worldly, sensual musical art form into the church is the trashing of over three hundred years of often-sanctified church music.

It seems as if the generation that grew up in the age of rebellion in Amer-ica (the '60s and '70s) not only want to bring their secular music into the sanctuary, but they want to dispense with most traditional church music, regardless of its beauty, spiritual honesty, and historical tradition. It's almost as if there is a perverse resistance to anything beautiful, quiet, introspective, and holy.

Could it be that the generation to which we are referring were so lit-tle exposed to beautiful music of any kind that they resist keeping it in the church because they do not understand or sense it?

How can one honestly say that screaming electric guitars, sexy sounding saxophones, throbbing electric basses, and clanging, banging loud drums ever be considered holy, worshipful or reverent?

A Moment of Truth

Sooner or later pastors, music and worship leaders, and elders of churches where this kind of music is glorified must ask themselves: *Is this a worshipful atmosphere? Are we polluting the sanctuary? Are people coming for a sensory experience rather than worship? Have we mistaken "getting high" on rock music with a true outbreak of the Holy Spirit?* Christ warns us in the Olivet Discourse (Matt. 24; Mark 13; and Luke 21) that the primary sign that will occur in the years just preceding His return will be *spiritual deception.*

Cleansing the Temple

It is bothersome to walk into a sanctuary to worship and be blasted out by a traveling semi-star Christian "artist," who has a table of CDs, T-shirts, etc. on sale in the lobby. What is this? Christ cleansed the temple twice. Why? Because many had turned it into a "den of thieves." He cleansed it to restore its holiness. We need to do the same today.

Whenever I've challenged the appropriateness of contemporary rock music being in the sanctuary, I'm always told, "They like it!" I'm here to tell you that is a *bald-face lie.* I challenge any music and worship leader or pastor to study the body language and participation of their congregation whenever the music is loud, repetitive, and overly syncopated.

Generally, over two-thirds of the congregation *do not participate,* they *endure.* Those who come to church to be entertained or to get "high" on the music are the only ones who "like" it. I challenge any pastor of a church where rock music is played in the sanctuary during a church service to honestly and objectively survey their congregation regarding this matter.

Lyrics vs. the Rest

Another lame excuse that I often hear is that the music is okay because it has "spiritual" lyrics. *The lyric can and will never overcome the emotional and physiological affects generated by the music.* I've heard demonically-driven so-called

Christian rock groups screaming at the top of their voice, jumping around stage, making sensual movements, dressed in a rebellious style . . . throwing in the name of "Jesus" every once in awhile, claiming that they are a good and "true" witness for our Lord, and they are attracting thousands of young listeners to Christ.

If they are attracting young listeners to Christ, then it is another Christ, and not the Christ of the Bible. The true church has never been concerned about numbers, only about souls. We all know that the true path is narrow. If it suddenly becomes very broad, we should begin to examine our policies concerning salvation.

Spiritual Warfare

Satan has used loud, repetitive music with sensual syncopated patterns for thousands of years to delude, overwhelm, and influence mankind. This is not a matter of opinion but of historical record. To see this kind of music enter the sanctuary on a regular basis must bring a particular cry of joy to Satan and his demons. There is no place on earth he tries harder to enter than a true worship service.

Pastors, music and worship leaders, elders, deacons, please search the Scriptures for justification for this kind of "entertainment" in the church. You will not find it. Search the historical traditions of the true church and you will not find it. Rock music is the first popular/secular musical style to overwhelm traditional church liturgy and replace it with sensual entertainment. The history of these phenomena is less than forty years old, and the church has been around for two thousand years!

A careful examination of the physiological effects of this kind of music is contrary to all that would lead one to a quiet, contemplative, and holy atmosphere appropriate to true worship.

Prophetic Fulfillment

By attending Christian rock concerts, does not one identify oneself with their ecumenism and their false doctrines and become a partaker of their evil deeds? (The Bible clearly teaches a theology of guilt by association— see 2 John 10–11). And since we will all be accountable to the Lord at the Bema Seat for our stewardship with the resources he has entrusted to us while on this earth, how can anyone possibly justify allocating any resources to the support of rock music?

—Tim Fisher, *The Battle for Christian Music*, 1992

In a positive way, the phenomena of rock music in the church is fulfillment of prophecy. Those who search the Scriptures honestly and diligently know that it has been predicted that in the last days there would be two churches: one devoted to Scripture and holiness, the other polluted by the world and occult and sensual practices. Which church do you serve, which do you belong to?

Paul gave the apostle in 2 Timothy one of the most accurate descriptions on the times in which we live:

> This know also, that in the last days perilous times shall come. For men shall be lovers of their own selves, covetous, boasters, proud, blasphemers, disobedient to parents, unthankful, unholy, Without natural affection, trucebreakers, false accusers, incontinent, fierce, despisers of those that are good, Traitors, heady, highminded, lovers of pleasures more than lovers of God; *Having a form of godliness, but denying the power thereof*: from such turn away.
>
> —2 Timothy 3:1–5

True Worship

Vladimir Lenin, the co-founder of communism and one of history's greatest experts on subversion and revolution said, *"One quick way to destroy a society is through its music."*

—*The Marxist Minstrels: A Handbook on Communist Subversion of Music*, American Christian College Press, 1974)

When we worship the God of the Bible as instructed, we are suddenly in the *pure atmosphere of Heaven itself.* The angels will join us in worship. We will not and must not use the rhythms and hypnotic musical techniques of the world or we will face *judgment* for our actions. We do not need music which excites us (fight-or-flight response) and makes us more aggressive and *less* able to concentrate on the Word of God. We must crucify our carnal nature, not strengthen it. We must relearn to worship God in spirit and in truth, *not in the flesh* (Phil. 3:3; John 4:24).

God does not live in noise and shouting, as Elijah learned. God is with those who are broken, contrite, and humble (Isa. 57:15). Scripture records an earlier rebellion, God's warning, and the rebuttal:

> Thus saith the LORD, Stand ye in the ways, and see, and *ask for the old paths, where is the good way, and walk therein,* and ye shall find rest for your souls. But they [rebellious, carnal, prideful Israel] said, We will not walk therein.
>
> —Jeremiah 6:16

Summary

Over 2,000 years *before the birth of Christ* the musical systems of China was both highly developed and central to its society. It was to this that the philosophers directed much of their attention. *Understanding its intrinsic power,* they carefully checked their music to make sure that it conveyed *eternal truths* and could influence man's character for the better.

—David Tame, *The Secret Power of Music* (Destiny Books), p. 34

I have tried to understand the power that this worldly music has over people and over many in the contemporary church. I believe it is a combination of naivete—not understanding the physiological, emotional, psychological, and spiritual fallout that comes from bringing the music of rebellion (rock)—and a form of pride into the sanctuary.

> To this end, tradition states that one [Chinese] emperor, by the name of Shun, would monitor the health of each of the provinces of this vast kingdom by simply examining the music they produced. *Course and sensual sounds indicated a sick society, one in need of his intervention and assistance.*
>
> —David Tame, *The Secret Power of Music,* pp. 13–14

Satan's biggest tool over all of us is pride. Man fell because of pride, and he still today spiritually deceives more non-believers and believers through pride than any other way, particularly in the church. Those of us in the church are aware of the too obvious sins, but pride, and particularly spiritual pride, is subtle, easily rationalized, and hard to resist.

Those who grew up in the two decades of rebellion in America, the '60s and '70s, are the most insistent that rock music replace traditional church music in the sanctuary. They want to bring their drug of choice into the Holy of Holies and toss out two thousand years of tradition. What a hold this music must have on them!

We cannot become part of the world to win the world. It will not work. It is not part of God's plan. God cannot make a "deal" with mammon (secular society) to win souls. The art of compromise does not apply in separating good from evil.

God calls us in these latter days to "come out from them!" (meaning secular society) not "go back in!" We are told in 1 John to "love not the things of the world" . . . which includes its music. The church understood the difference between sacred and secular music for almost two thousand years. Why the recent and sudden urgency to change?

To those who support this type of music in worship, I challenge you to justify your support of rock music in the sanctuary spiritually, emotionally, intellectually, culturally—it is logically not possible. I also ask you to honestly search the Scriptures and ask if it is not pride that is ruling in this area. Rock 'n roll is named for the act of fornication. How can that style of music be appropriate for worship? The apostle Paul tells us in Philippians 4:8:

> Finally, brethren, whatsoever things are true, whatsoever things are honest, whatsoever things are just, whatsoever things are pure, whatsoever things are lovely, whatsoever things are of good report; if there be any virtue, and if there be any praise, think on these things.

To those of you who do not support this music in the sanctuary, please have the courage to tell your church leaders. Courage is one of the true characteristics of being a Christian. If the church fails to listen, seek another church. *Do not support a church where true worship is impossible and the music is repugnant and contrary to all definitions of holiness.* Ask your pastor to read the above Philippians passage of Scripture along with Ephesians 4:17–24 and other scriptures warning us about becoming part of the world . . . and how that applies to rock music. You have a right to know. Your eternal destiny may ride on it.

Demonology 101

The Dark Side

Because of my years wandering around in false religions and cults, I am more sensitive and aware of the power, cunning, and deceptive practices of the dark side, the demonic side, of the invisible. The Christian church today is incredibly naïve regarding the forces of evil and their fanatical desire to destroy every believer in Christ and every Jew on this planet.

They have had thousands of years to practice manipulating and deceiving mankind. Appealing to our innate pride has always worked well, as well as our sensual appetites for sex, money, power, and food. Today they are more active than ever before for six reasons:

1. The church has not learned how to protect itself from these invisible forces and as a result are vulnerable to attack, temptation, and deception.
2. The body of Christ, for the most part, is almost biblically illiterate. Scripture teaches that "the people perish for lack of knowledge," spiritual knowledge.
3. The moral relativism of today's society; where there is no right, there is no wrong, and no one is held responsible for their behavior (it's always someone else's fault) has crept into the church. *Christians are afraid to take a stand against the forces of evil, even in their own churches.*
4. Ambitious, charismatic, but spiritually immature pastors have built megachurches on false doctrines, pointing to their worldly "success" as a sign they are "blessed" by God. Nothing could be further from the truth.
5. The incredible power of music. Music can affect us physically, emotionally, and spiritually, even if we resist, because it triggers an emotional response in the brain before our conscious sensors can evaluate and ratify its worth. Satan knows this. In Ezekiel 28 and Isaiah 14, two chapters

that describe Satan in great detail, we discover that before his rebellion and fall *he was in charge of music.*

6. Christ warned us that spiritual deception would be the greatest challenge to the church in His important and lengthy message called the *Olivet Discourse* in Matthew 24–25, Mark 13, and Luke 21. *The only way not to be deceived is to know your Bible* and have a healthy respect for the subtle powers of the forces of darkness in manipulating mankind since the fall in Genesis 3.

Satan's Army

Satan, our primary adversary, has an army. It's made up of fallen angels and demons. Many believe demons to be fallen angels. Others believe demons to be disembodied spirits from the Antediluvian period (pre-flood). Either way, they are soldiers in Satan's army and stand ready on a twenty-four-hour basis to do battle with mankind. Their primary targets are Christians and Jews.

It's one thing to see their evil influence and possession of the naïve in secular society. It's another to actually see and hear these demonically driven "artists" fire up their high-decibel amplified instruments, stroll onto the stage in the sanctuary of our churches dressed like the homeless, with an arrogant attitude in a supposedly sacred Christian worship service. Can a bad tree give good fruit?

The English word "demon" is a translation of the Greek word *daemon*. It is mistranslated as "devils" in the King James Bible. It should always be translated as "demons." The Greek word in the New Testament comes from the root *da* which means "to know." The word demon means "a knowing one."

Demons have supernatural knowledge of mankind, families, churches, countries, and individuals. They have been roaming the earth for thousands of years. They are intelligent, well informed, and very cunning. *You will never be able to outsmart them.* They are sly and crafty. Yet, even a baby Christian can send them fleeing by *pleading the blood of Jesus* over himself, his family, etc., and rebuking them in the name of *Jesus*. You need Christ, Scripture, a solid local church, and knowledge in fighting these supernatural enemies.

The Bible teaches that demons formed a federation of evil under the leadership of Satan, once called "Lucifer." The Bible speaks of the "devil and his angels" (Matt. 25:41). Scripture also tells us that Satan already has a kingdom (Matt. 12:26–27) and that the demons are his army. Demons are his agents and emissaries. His kingdom is very strong and very large.

Only through the powerful name of Jesus Christ and knowledge gleaned from Scripture can we learn how to defeat the forces of evil. You see, Satan and his demons are beyond hope. God already condemns them to an eternity of punishment in Hell. Consequently they fight hard, desperately hoping that in some miraculous way they will succeed in unseating God and winning control of not only planet earth but the universe as well.

The devil took Jesus up into a very high place and showed Him all the kingdoms of the world and the glory of them. Then Satan said to our Lord, "All these things will I give thee, if thou wilt fall down and worship me" (Matt. 4:8–9). There is a similar passage in Luke 4:5–6 where the devil adds, "All this power will I give thee, and the glory of them: *for that is delivered unto me; and to whomsoever I will I give it.*"

The devil controls the nations of the world. There is only one nation that God has a special covenant with, and that is Israel. All other nations are subject to Satan's control. He's also called "the prince of the power of the air" (Eph. 2:2) and "the god of this world" (2 Cor. 4:4). Another title for Satan is Beelzebub, which has been mistranslated as "the Lord of the Flies." It should translate: "the Lord that flies."

Remember that Satan is a created being and that God is still sovereign. God is supreme. But through the fall of Adam and Eve Satan has gained control (the deed) to planet earth.

Demon Possession

Man has three spiritual states: he can be in control of his own mind and spirit, even though he is constantly being influenced and deceived by Satan; he can be controlled through the indwelling of the Holy Spirit—if he chooses Christ as his Lord and Savior and confesses his sins; or he can be in some instances be *controlled by demons:*

> When the even was come, they brought unto him [Jesus] many that were possessed with devils: and he cast out the spirits with his word. . . .
> —Matthew 8:16

And when he was come to the other side into the country of the Gerge-senes, there met him two possessed with devils, coming out of the tombs, exceeding fierce, so that no man might pass by that way.

—Matthew 8:28

And it came to pass, as we went to prayer, a certain damsel possessed with a spirit of divination met us. . . .

—Acts 16:16

Latter Days

Scripture indicates that Satan and his demons will step up their influence over nations, societies, the arts, people, and events in the last days. After a great deal of research I have come to the conclusion that contemporary rock music is mostly demon-driven and its main thrust is the corruption of young people and the Christian church. Major Christian leaders like Dave Wilkerson, Dave Hunt, John MacArthur, Dr. James Dobson, Dr. D, James Kennedy, and reformed former Christian rock musicians like Dan Lucarini (get his book: *Why I Left the Contemporary Christian Music Movement*), and many others agree.

Now the Spirit speaketh expressly, that in the latter times some shall depart from the faith, giving heed to seducing spirits, and doctrines of devils.

—1 Timothy 4:1

We will see an increasing influence of demons on world-leaders:

For they are the spirits of [devils], *working miracles*, which go forth unto the *kings of the earth and of the whole world.* . . .

—Revelation 16:14

But evil men and seducers shall wax worse and worse, deceiving, and being deceived.

—2 Timothy 3:13

Physical Maladies

Demons can (on the unsaved) inflict physical maladies. The gospels are full of examples of Christ healing a person whose disability was supernatural:

And his fame went throughout all Syria: and they brought unto him all sick people that were taken with divers diseases and torments, and those which were possessed with devils [demons], and those which were lunatick, and those that had the palsy; and he [Christ] *healed them.*

—Matthew 4:24

In Matthew 17:15–18 a distraught father approached Jesus and said:

Lord, have mercy on my son: for he is lunatick, and sore vexed: for ofttimes he falleth into the fire, and oft into the water. . . . And Jesus rebuked the devil [demon]; and he departed out of him: and the child was cured from that very hour.

Note: In every instance in dealing with demons, Jesus first told them to be quiet and then He cast them out in *His name.* We should follow the same script if ever confronted with demon possession. All the power over them rests in *His name.*

Supernatural Strength
Demonically possessed people can often manifest supernatural strength:

And when he was come to the other side into the country of the Gerge-senes, there met him two possessed with devils, coming out of the tombs, *exceeding fierce,* so that no man might pass by that way.

—Matthew 8:28

Children of Disobedience
The "children of disobedience" are those who have heard the gospel message and have rejected it or modified it to suit their own lusts:

Wherein in time past ye walked according to the course of this world, ac-cording to the *prince of the power of the air,* the spirit *that now* worketh in the *children of disobedience.*

—Ephesians 2:2

Actually anyone who has not surrendered his or her life to Jesus Christ can be spiritually deceived. In fact, Christ said in the Olivet Discourse (Matt. 24, Mark 13, Luke 21) that *even the very elect* are subject to spiritual deception in the "last days." The devil tempts, twists, and leads people into sin. Those who do not know Jesus Christ as Lord and Savior are in *"the snare of the devil, and are easily taken captive by him at his will"* (2 Tim. 2:26)

Paul the apostle reminds us often that people are not the real enemy; it is the supernatural force behind the person or groups that is the real enemy:

> For we wrestle not against flesh and blood, but against principalities, against powers, against the rulers of the darkness of this world, against spiritual wickedness in high places.
>
> —Ephesians 6:12

That is why Christ could say from the cross, "Father, forgive them for they know not what they do," and Stephen and other martyrs of the faith could actually be asking God to forgive those that were taking his or her life. We can only learn to "love" or have mercy on our enemies when we realize that they are merely *slaves of the devil.*

Demonic Phenomena

1. They inflict disease (not all disease, but certain diseases) (Job 1:5–10; Matt. 9:33, 12:22; Luke 9:37–42, 13:11,16).
2. They can cause mental disorders (Mark 5:4–5; Luke 8:35).
3. They lead many into moral depravity, decay, licentiousness (Matt. 10:1, 12:43; Mark 1:23–27, 3:11, 5:2–13; Luke 4:33,36, 6:18, 8:29; Acts 5:16, 8:7; Rev. 16:13).
4. They create false doctrine (1 Kings 22:21–23; 2 Thess 2:2; 1 Tim. 4:1).
5. They harass, oppress, oppose God's children (Eph. 6:12).
6. They sometimes possess humans or animals (Matt. 4:24; Mark 5:8–14; Luke 8:2; Acts 8:7, 16:16.).
7. They are often unwittingly used by God to carry out His plans (Judg. 9:23; 1 Sam 16:14; Ps. 78:49). *God will specifically use them during the Tribulation Period, giving some miraculous powers* (Rev. 9:1–12, 16:13–16).
8. They are the force behind all false religions, philosophy, occult practices such as astrology, necromancy, etc. (Isa. 47:13; Acts 16:16). No one truly knows the future but God. God gives us all the guidance we need to prepare for the future in Scripture. Everything else is *false and misleading.*

9. They use certain styles of music to gain control of the listener's mind, to plant seeds of rebellion, trigger sensual behavior, and encourage drug use.

What We Need to Know and Remember

1. Demonology reveals the real nature of sin and the depth and ruin to which it may bring the individual human soul. The end is always eternal destruction, for those deceived as well as those doing the deception.

2. Knowing the basics of spiritual warfare will inspire a healthy fear and hatred of evil in all its forms. Although appearing innocent, the goal of demonic seduction is enslavement, punishment, degradation, and eventual eternal damnation for whoever they first seduce and then attack.

3. Christ is the only hope in surviving a demonized world and eventually escaping it. *Submission to Christ is our only way out.*

4. Being trained in spiritual warfare will bring greater appreciation for personal salvation and protection. The devil and his demons cannot be saved. Their fate is already sealed. *Keep your eye on the ball. Eternal salvation and spiritual protection while living on this sin-filled planet must be your primary goals.*

> Looking back on the early years of rock and roll now, I can see why the adults were scared. The screams, the ecstatic states, the hysteria—this music had a power that adults didn't understand. We didn't even understand it ourselves, but we weren't as scared of it as they were. When I think back on the tens of thousands of garage bands that sprang up as rock took hold I realize now it was one of *the most powerful explosions of art this country has ever experienced.*
>
> —Mickey Hart (drummer with the Grateful Dead),
> *Drumming at the Edge of Magic*, 1997, p. 228

5. Have a healthy respect for the deceptive powers of Satan. Be aware that his primary target is the church. If he can weaken the church he gains power. Understand that music is one of his primary ways to gain access and eventual control of the human mind.

6. Memorize scripture that can be used to resist Satan. Remember Mat-

thew 4; Christ answered Satan each time with appropriate scripture. Learn to fight!

Jesus Is Lord

Jesus is Lord. He is Lord of all. If we are one of His lambs *no one can snatch us out of His hand.* However, unless we learn the basic techniques of spiritual warfare we will be subject to individual and collective mass deception, temptation, and oppression. The Bible says, "The joy of the Lord is our strength!" Be watchful. When we begin to lose our joy we can almost always be assured that Satan is once again tempting us.

Know Your Enemy

Have a healthy respect for the power Satan has over the unsaved and the constant attempts to deceive the elect. Understand that spiritual warfare is a daily battle. No believer is immune from Satan's wiles. He will constantly test us, looking for weaknesses. We must call on the only power greater than his, the power of Jesus Christ, and confess thankfully that "greater is he [Jesus] that is within us than he [Satan] that is against us."

Christ told us in John 17 that one of His primary reasons for coming to earth (besides providing a way out of man's separation from God through Jesus' sacrifice on the cross) was to *destroy to works of the devil.*

Take a Stand

Are we helping to weaken Satan or strengthen him? Prayer, confession of sin, Bible studies, and sanctified worship—all weaken his hold on mankind and the church. Allowing him to sneak into the sanctuary through the music and corrupt the offering of worship unto an almighty God is one of Satan's primary goals. *Don't let it happen!*

Demonology 102

Wherefore we would have come unto you, even I Paul, once and again; *but Satan hindered us.*

—1 Thessalonians 1:18

If Satan could have that effect on God's main man, what can he do to hinder our walk with Christ? Very little in fact, if we really understand the basic rules of spiritual warfare. A great deal if we don't.

For this cause, when I could no longer forbear, I sent to know your faith, lest by some means *the tempter have tempted you, and our labour be in vain.*

—1 Thessalonians 3:5

What is the enemy trying to tempt us to do or not to do? First of all, Satan through his army of demons, will work very hard to keep us from (1) praying, (2) studying the Word of God, and (3) true sanctified worship.

The Rules of Spiritual Warfare

After our salvation in Jesus Christ, which guarantees us eventual victory, we must practice the basics of our faith: prayer, Bible study (which includes the memorization of key verses), and true worship, where Christ is lifted up, not the pastor or the choir or the guest artist or evangelist.

After the basics, we must learn to fight. We must learn how the enemy thinks. We must know what resources he has, and what resources he claims to have, but doesn't.

Remember that Christ called Satan "the father of lies." Christ also called him a "murderer." He doesn't operate alone. He has a hierarchy of fallen angels that do his bidding. They are the principalities, powers, and demons that the Bible tells us about.

Demons are part of the invisible army of Satan. They harrass believers and try to enter to possess or influence non-believers. They are spiritual parasites. However, they cannot enter the mind of a believer to influence and control beyond his or her level of consciousness *without the consent of the person.*

No one in their right mind would voluntarily surrender control of their mind to a spiritual parasite. The key words are "right mind." Under the influence of drugs, illicit sex, perversion, drunkenness, extreme rage, or extreme fright, sometimes a person can unwittingly open a contact point in their subconscious mind to demons. God can also use demons to discipline and to test our spiritual growth, as He did with Job, or discipline the backslider and those departing from the faith:

> This charge I commit unto thee, son Timothy, according to the prophecies which went before on thee, that thou by them mightest *war a good warfare;* Holding faith, and a good conscience; which some having put away concerning faith have made shipwreck: 20 Of whom is Hymenaeus and Alexander; whom *I have delivered unto Satan, that they may learn not to blaspheme.*
>
> —1 Timothy 1:18–20

The Occult

Meddling in occult practices such as a Ouiji board, the game Dungeons and Dragons, astrology, necromancy (contacting the dead through a medium), witchcraft, or devil worship, and listening regularly to heavy metal, gothic, and punk rock music can bring about temporary or permanent possession for the unsaved. Once Satan gets a foothold in your mind, he will work to enlarge it and weaken your will to resist.

False Religions

> Now the Spirit speaketh expressly, that in the latter times some shall depart from the faith, giving heed to *seducing spirits, and doctrines of devils.*
>
> —1 Timothy 4:1

All false religions are demon-inspired. Submitting yourself to a false religion is to offer yourself for possession and control by dangerous, dark spirits and forces. Remember that there is a demon behind all idols, cults, cult leaders, all designed to deceive and mislead mankind. For instance, those given a *mantra* to chant while meditating, as are all initiates in Transcendental Meditation, Self-Realization Fellowship, and other Hindu yoga cults, are actually chanting the ancient Sanskrit name of one of the thousands of Hindu demons to come and "live" in you.

Apostate Christianity

Apostate Christianity begins when any Christian church disregards the Bible as the final authority and guide in all matters pertaining to the faith. Today we are living in one of the greatest periods of apostasy in the history of the church:

> For the time will come when they will not endure sound doctrine; but after their own lusts shall they heap to themselves teachers, having itching ears; 4 And they shall *turn away their ears from the truth, and shall be turned unto fables.*
>
> —2 Timothy 4:3–4

Jesus as Lord

> Beloved, believe not every spirit, but *try the spirits* whether they are of God: because many false prophets are gone out into the world. Hereby know ye the Spirit of God: *Every spirit that confesseth that Jesus Christ is come in the flesh is of God:* And every spirit that confesseth not that Jesus Christ is come in the flesh is not of God: and this is that spirit of *antichrist*, whereof ye have heard that it should come; *and even now already is it in the world.*
>
> —1 John 4:1–3

John the apostle gives us a litmus test regarding deceptive spirits. *Jesus was and is God in the flesh.* Any other interpretation is a deceptive spirit. Christian Scientists believe Jesus was a "force" we can all tap into; Mormons believe that Jesus and Satan were twins; Jehovah's Witnesses believe Jesus was an angel, and so on.

As C. S. Lewis so clearly states in his important work, *Mere Christianity,* Jesus was God in the flesh, or the greatest spiritual deceiver who ever lived, or a madman. No other position can be taken *based on Scripture.* Those who tell you Jesus never claimed to be divine are liars. Read John 8 as well as many other passages where Jesus claimed divinity. In fact, the real reason the Jews demanded his crucifixion was because Jesus claimed to be *the Son of God*.

Unnatural Fears and Phobias

For God hath *not* given us the *spirit of fear*; but of *power*, and of *love*, and of a *sound mind*.

—2 Timothy 1:7

Sometimes Satan will make us unnaturally afraid of normal circumstances and events, places, people, etc. Please note that in this scriptural passage, God reveals to Timothy that there is actually a *spirit of fear*. We know that spirit is active when normal events, places, and people suddenly bring about an unnatural fear. If and when that happens, *claim this scripture and rebuke the spirit in Jesus' name. Order it to leave in Jesus' name and not come back.*

Crime

Perpetrators of particularly vicious crimes are often under the control of demons. Sometimes victims are exposed to these dark forces as well. This is particularly true in the area of spousal and child abuse, including pedophilia and incest. We all read in the paper daily or see on the news examples of horrible crimes that could not be done by any normal person in their right mind.

Those who are unreasonably violent to animals, children, women, or the elderly are opening themselves up to demonic control. In tracing the careers of mass murderers, one often finds a gradual escalation of violence that often becomes uncontrollable. Learning to have mercy and learning to care for one another is not just an unrealistic platitude. It is a necessary practice to live a normal life and avoid demonic contamination.

Lying, Deceiving

Lying is a serious sin in the Bible. It is usually listed just after idolatry. Lying is not only deceiving others, but deceiving yourself as well. A strong condemnation regarding lying and deception in the early church is given in Acts 5 when Ananias and Sapphira lied to the Holy Spirit and suffered death as a result. *When you lie, you join forces with Satan's army. It's his most used weapon of deception.*

Sexual Perversion

God destroyed two cities called Sodom and Gomorrah in the Old Testament (Gen. 19) because of the *acceptance* of homosexuality as an alternative lifestyle. Homosexuality is just one of many abhorrent sexual practices. Pedophilia, bestiality, incest, group sex, pornography, sadism, adultery, fornication, voyeurism—all are the devil's tools to debase mankind and destroy the sanctity of marriage and the family.

Our culture has become obsessed with sex. Madison Avenue advertising agencies discovered years ago they could sell almost anything with sex. Consequently we are bombarded with titillating sexual images day and night. We are becoming a modern Sodom with open acceptance of homosexuality as "normal." Will God judge us? I believe He will if our nation does not turn from its wicked ways. God still opens His hand of forgiveness, as He did to the ancient Hebrews:

> And now, Israel, what doth the LORD thy God require of thee, but to fear the LORD thy God, to walk in all his ways, and to love him, and to serve the LORD thy God with all thy heart and with all thy soul, To keep the commandments of the LORD, and his statutes, which I command thee this day for thy good?
>
> —Deuteronomy 10:12–13

Leviticus 18 describes all the above, and even more sexually aberrant behavior. The chapter closes by telling us that *such were the normal practices of the Egyptians and Canaanites.* As a result, both ancient cultures were destroyed. God warns us in this chapter that the land itself will "vomit out" the people who engage regularly in this kind of behavior. Will we be "vomited out" in America? Pray for revival!

The Arts

Music, drama, dance, and literature can also contribute to exposure to the dark forces. Much of today's so-called modern art is demonically inspired. The dark ugliness and violence as well as the hopelessness much of these so-called "arts" produce can have a deleterious affect on young minds.

Rock Music

In Africa musicians are never possessed by the spirits they call down with

their rhythms, so what possesses our [rock] audience I can never know.
But I feel its effects. From the stage you can feel it happening—group
mind, entrancement, find your own word for it—then they lock up; you
can feel it; you can feel the energy roaring off them.

—Mickey Hart, *Drumming at the Edge of Magic*, p. 230

Rock music is from the pit of Hell. It was birthed during a moral low point
in American culture, the 1960s . . . free dope, free sex, free music, question
authority, "if it feels good, do it!" Out of this nest of vipers came rock music.
Now this loud, pagan, hypnotizing music is in the sanctuaries of our churches, and modern pastors and church leaders are pronouncing it as okay.

Rock music is demonically driven. Changing the lyrics to something
"spiritual" but keeping the same arrogant "in-your-face" attitude, clothes,
and loud presentation does not make it okay.

Isn't it sad when you see parents reliving their lives through their children. To a certain extent, demons try to do the same thing: relive their sordid
and depraved lives through others. In this manner they are not only able to
turn the person they are influencing away from the one true God of the universe and His Son, Jesus Christ, they are also able to degrade their hosts and
lead them to do terrible things they could never do in their "right" mind.

The Middle East

I believe that modern-day Palestine is one of the most demonically inhabited
places on earth. The constant cycle of violence is hypnotic to demons and
attracts them by the thousands. Another attraction is the devil's desire to
totally wipe out Israel and all the Jews in the world so Christ will have no
country or people to be King of when He returns.

I remember on my most recent trip to Israel standing in the ruins of
the ancient temple of the northern kingdom of Israel after the nation had
broken into two parts, separating the southern kingdom of Judah from the
northern kingdom of Israel around 940 b.c. The northern kingdom, called
"Israel," quickly returned to the ancient Egyptian gods (the golden calf)
under their leader Jeroboam. After repeated warnings from God's faithful
prophets that the northern kingdom faced God's judgment for their open
idolatry, the northern kingdom was conquered by Assyria and most of the
people remaining alive were taken into captivity and spread throughout the

vast Assyrian Empire (722 b.c.). As I stood on the recently unearthed site of the northern kingdom's idolatrous temple, one could still *feel* the evil presence in that place!

I also believe that Islam is one of the most demonically-driven religions in the world. Its founder, Mohammed, was a documented demon-possessed pedophile (see the Hadith and the Koran). In approved Islamic bibliographies we read about the struggle he had with this "presence" that grabbed him in such a way that he felt "crushed." This was the same "presence" that gave him his supposed sacred writings. He later called this presence the angel Gabriel, but earlier in his life he said he was not sure it was not a demon (which the Muslims call a *djinn*.)

Summary

The contemporary Christian church today is so naïve about the power and purpose of demons. There are few sermons about Heaven, even fewer about Hell, and *never* about demons. Christ himself in the Olivet Discourse (Matt. 24–25; Mark 13; Luke 21) said that *spiritual deception* would be the primary sign of the times just prior to His return. We are seeing that today, outside and within the church.

End-time prophecy in the Bible tells us over and over that spiritual deception will increase in "the last days." Jesus warned that even "the very elect" could be deceived. We need to take spiritual warfare seriously and not laugh it off as some aberrant idea exaggerating the dangers in the spiritual world. On the other hand, we need to claim victory, knowing our Lord has already defeated Satan on the cross. We are just part of a mopping up operation . . . but one that will challenge our knowledge of scripture in learning how to fight and win. Nowhere is spiritual deception more blatant than in today's "Christian" rock music.

"Jesus loves me, this I know, for the Bible tells me so." This old children's song summarizes the entire Bible. Jesus does love us. Jesus will protect us. Jesus will lead us toward the light, but we must learn how to defend ourselves, our family, our church, and our nation against the forces of darkness. Our training manual is the Bible. All we need to know to succeed in the battling the forces of darkness are contained therein . . . so get busy! Study! Learn how to fight!

Adrenaline: Hormone of Fear

The human body has its own emergency set of procedures which have protected us for thousands of years. One of these devices is the body-produced hormone called *adrenaline*. Two small glands, the adrenal glands, sit on top of our kidneys. When the brain sends a signal to this gland that danger is present, the gland secretes a miraculous body-produced drug into the blood stream that gives our body extra energy to fight or run, and also sharpens the survival skills of our mind by making us more hyperalert and hyper-aggressive.

The stimulus that triggers this automatic response of the adrenal glands can be visual, auditory, or physical. We can see danger, hear danger, or even feel it. We could be suddenly bumped or bitten. Even our powerful imagination can trigger this response by visualization—watching a play or movie—or hearing the standard sudden, repetitive, sharp sounds from the rock drummer which the brain always interprets as a potential threat.

Physical feelings include the speeding and contraction of the heart, a feeling of heat in the stomach, and a feeling of jitteriness in the muscles. It may be hard to sit still, or keep from moving. *There is a thrill or elation that goes with this feeling.* We suddenly feel powerful and totally in charge. The mind is under control of the emotions, and logic takes a backseat to feelings.

Certain skills call for a controlled use of adrenaline stimulation. For instance, author David Morell in his recent spy novel *The Protector* explains how special forces in the military use certain repetitive but dangerous exercises to stimulate adrenaline until the individual begins to feel comfortable with the stimulus and eventually comes to crave it. War may be "hell," but the adrenaline-rush of combat is something no soldier will ever forget. The same is said for professional athletes, entertainers, politicians, race car drivers, law enforcement agencies, and gang-bangers.

Put a parachute on someone and tell that person to leap out of a plane at twenty thousand feet, he's going to be terrified. It's a potentially life-threatening activity and one that's totally unfamiliar.

But train that person in small increments, teach him how to jump off increasingly high platforms into a swimming pool. Then teach him how to jump from even higher platforms wearing a bungee harness that simulates the feel of a parachute. Then show him how to jump from small planes at reasonable altitudes.

Gradually increase the size and power of the planes and the height of the jump. By the time he leaps from that plane at twenty thousand feet, he's going to feel the same speeding and contraction of the heart, the same burning in the stomach, the same jitteriness in the muscles as before.

This time, though, he's *not terrified.* He knows how to minimize the risk, and he's experienced hundreds of similar activities. What he feels instead of fear is the *sharp focus of an athlete ready to spring into action.* His adrenaline is affecting him the same way it always did. But his mind knows how to control it and to appreciate its constructive effects.

—David Morrell, *The Protector,* p. 93

The speeding and the contraction of the heart cause a greater output of blood to reach muscles and prepare them for extreme action. The faster breath rate causes more oxygen to get to muscles. The *liver creates glucose, increasing the amount of sugar in the blood.* At the same time, more fatty acids circulate. Both the sugar and the fatty acids become instant fuel, creating greater energy and stamina.

Professional athletes, race car drivers, dancers, rock musicians, politicians, and law enforcement personnel are trained to separate their fear from the adrenaline rush. These professionals rely on the adrenaline rush to get them ready, but they have minimized the fear through repetitive training.

Unfortunately we can get addicted to the rush. *This addiction can be as intense and hard to break as addiction to alcohol, smoking, cocaine, heroin, or methamphetamines. Loud rock music can produce the same adrenaline rush and can be just as addictive, if not more so, because it is so cleverly hidden.*

Although there are long periods of inactivity in each of the dangerous professions, even the waiting for danger and excitement can trigger the rush.

Are you looking forward to going to church to get a rock music rush, or to worship? You can't have it both ways.

Today, millions of teenagers are adrenaline rush addicts. They have learned to overstimulate their adrenal glands to receive the giant rush. It's conscience soothing and it gets mom and dad off their back when the music is "Christian" rock. Everybody wins.

Aggression

Today there are mosh pits at Christian rock concerts. What's a mosh pit? Unable to control the need to bang into someone, those most high on the music gather in front of the bandstand and literally bang into each other. Bouncers are stationed around the area ready to extract anyone who gets too violent in their behavior. *The mosh pit is a natural byproduct of rock music.*

There are few big rock festivals anymore. The aggression released is often hard to control, even with the mosh pit escape valve. Too many people have been crushed, hit, burned, or trampled. Major rock festivals can and often do result in riots, antisocial behavior, or waves of destructiveness toward the immediate environment and others. The *Rolling Stone's* rock concert in Altamonte, California, years ago saw a murder in front of the bandstand, in spite of the Hell's Angels motorcycle club serving as security guards. The insurance today is too prohibitive for another Woodstock.

Today the only groups that can get away with major rock festivals are the Christian rock group promoters. Even with the supposed "good" kids, security guards abound and the mosh pit is a must as an escape valve for uncontrollable aggression. This is supposed to be a religious experience?

Volume and Violence

Today the entertainment industry has combined two major stimulants artificially in MTV, VH-1, and films: volume and violence. Those witnessing this new pairing of extreme visual violence and loud rock music usually get a "rush" and even become more addicted to his deadly combination. In fact, a new Hollywood entertainment genre has been created, called "slasher" films, and rap—a degenerate form of rock music—now touts "gangsta" rap.

Today, fourth graders whose naïve parents let their kids watch MTV or VH1 or buy the CDs or DVDs are apparently numb to the conditioning of the lyrics where the "gangsta" rapper attacks law enforcement officials, boasts about carrying a gun, and calls females "bitches" and "hos," or where some diabolical stalker hunts down and kills in a very dramatic manner many of the characters in a film. Even though the stalker is usually destroyed (or disappears only to reappear in a sequel) the damage is done.

Christ warned us that one of the signs of the last days preceding His return would be the increasing love of violence. He compared the times just before He comes back to the Antediluvian times of Noah in Genesis 6 where God indicates that violence was an addiction among that crowd.

Health Issues
Overstimulation of the adrenal glands can have many serious effects on health, particularly later in life. The overstimulation can:

1. Weaken the immune system
2. Weaken the heart
3. Lead to diabetes
4. Damage the nervous system
5. Cause chronic depression alternating with outbreaks of violent behavior.
6. Lead to obesity; the mind wants massive amounts of food to feed the energy levels necessary when "high."
7. Weaken response to real danger due to overstimulation.

Summary
The uncontrolled use of loud, sharp music in film soundtracks, the constant emphasis on gratuitous violence in books, television, films, and plays, and the dramatic enhancement of the news have all contributed to a society that has overstimulated its "fight or flight" response that nature built into our bodies and minds as a protective device.

This situation can weaken the nation as a whole, making it more vulnerable to outside aggressive nations who have not damaged their bodies, minds, and nervous systems in this manner. It's bad enough we have to hear and see this degenerate form of entertainment in our society. It's even worse to see it creep into our churches and into acceptable entertainment for Christian youth, although the Bible predicted that this would happen (2 Tim. 3:1–5).

Rhythm

Music is the effort we make to explain to ourselves how the mind works.

—Mickey Hart, *Drumming at the Edge of Magic,* p. 118

There are seven parts to music: rhythm, form, melody, countermelody, harmony, texture (tone quality, chord voicings), and style (tempo, dynamics, and articulation). These seven characteristics are listed in importance; in fact, you can have a musical performance with just the first two: rhythm and form.

Rhythmic Sensitivity

He who makes a mistake is still our friend; he who adds to, or shortens, a melody is still our friend; but he who violates a rhythm unawares can never be our friend.

—Arab proverb

Listeners are much more sensitive to rhythm than any other aspect of music. Our bodies are walking, breathing, speaking, rhythm machines. All of our automatic nervous systems—respiratory, circulatory, digestive, endocrine, and pulmonary—are in a continuous state of rhythmic activity. From a kinesthetic standpoint we move, speak, sleep, exercise, sneeze, eliminate, and even sleep rhythmically. The human body is amazing. One of the reasons our species has been able to survive major climate or environmental changes is our ability to adapt quickly to environmental changes. Man is in a constant state of homeostasis; in other words, subconsciously our body, mind, and emotions are constantly adapting to our environment.

Power of Rhythm

Military drums play music designed to make your feet take you where your head never would. Music is as dangerous as gunpowder.

—Naomi Orr

Throughout military history drums have been used to gradually enrage soldiers, helping them overcome their fear of death by beginning the drumbeats
slowly and repetitiously, then gradually increasing their volume, intensity,
and speed.

The power of rhythm is unbelievable. A military unit marching across
a suspension bridge must not march in step. The sympathetic vibrations of
all the soldiers' feet coming down at the same time could and would bring
the bridge down. Sports stadiums must be built with sound baffles or barriers that limit the power of sympathetic vibrations from the fans: stomping
their feet in rhythm, shouting in rhythm, etc., could negatively affect the
structure.

The Occult Power of Rhythm

> Africans, particularly West Africans, believe that the spirits ride the
> drumbeat down into the body of the dancers, who then begin the erratic
> shaking movements of the possessed.
>
> —Mickey Hart, *Drumming at the Edge of Magic*, p. 201

George Otis, Jr., well-known businessman, Christian author, traveler, and
speaker, in his book *The Twilight Labyrinth* (Chosen Books, 1997), exposes
the fact that demonic religions and cults throughout the known world *all* use
certain rhythm patterns and sounds to "call up" their local demons, who then
take possession of someone there (the demon's chosen medium or "channeler") who then precedes to give "supernatural" prophecies to those attending.

> During a possession consciousness is said to leave and go wandering while
> the spirit is in residence—typically they have no memory of anything that
> has happened and couldn't begin to tell you what the possessing spirit says
> through them.
>
> —George Otis, Jr., *The Twilight Labyrinth*, p. 202

Surprisingly, Mickey Hart, former drummer with the *Grateful Dead*, in
his popular book *Drumming at the Edge of Magic*, supports the research of
George Otis:

> Great care must be taken that only the correct spirit takes up residence.
> This was accomplished with *the drum. Particular rhythms are supposed to*

attract particular spirits. An *Orisha* (demon god) like *Shango* (popular West African, Caribbean, and Latin American demon god) *only comes when he hears his rhythm.*

—Hart, p. 204

Imagine the soundscape fifty thousand years ago. Noise meant danger, possibly death, an understanding rooted in the oldest parts of the brain, in the fight-or-flight programs that activate the adrenals, preparing the organism for immediate action. This is what the Hindus knew on a cosmic scale; there *is terror in noise and in that terror there is also power.*

—Mickey Hart, *Drumming at the Edge of Magic*, p. 12

There seems to be a morbid fascination on the part of major rock groups with the occult. For instance on the *Rolling Stone's* occult "Goat's Head Soup," they incorporate actual recording excerpts from voodoo ceremonies.

John Lennon, co-leader of the *Beatles* said in a *Rolling Stone* interview that

. . . rock & roll gets through to people because of its *voodoo* beat. Because it is primitive enough and has no bull, really, the best stuff, and it gets through to you because of its beat. *Go to the jungle and they have the rhythm* and it goes throughout the world and it's as simple as that.

Musicologist *John Chernoff* studied drumming in Africa, even participating in animal sacrifices and other pagan ceremonies to appease the drum spirits. After these demonic ceremonies, he claimed his arms did not tire and he "seemed never to make a mistake." Turnoff noted the close connection between the voodoo beat in African cult drumming and rock and roll:

Great drummers, aficionados, and scholars can trace the rhythms of the Latin dance halls of New York to Cuba and Brazilian cults and then all the way back to primitive, tribal West Africa.

—Chernoff, *African Rhythm and African Sensibility*, p. 29

Nothing New under the Sun

The ancient Greeks had two types of religious worship. The first type v serious, idealistic, inspirational music, usually vocal, accompanied by the sounds of the hand-held harp. The god most celebrated this way was Apollo. The second was ribald, bawdy, rowdy, lustful, sensual, and involved wild celebrations often degenerating into drunken orgies. The music was percussive, loud, and repetitive, and a wind popular instrument called the *aulos* had an uncanny sound much like the wailing of today's electric guitar. The god most celebrated this way was Bacchus. *Both religious types of celebrations were deemed necessary to balance man's nature.* Both were considered cathartic and purifying.

Music and Trance

Gilbert Rouget's excellent book *Music and Trance,* in his chapter on the ancient Greeks, points out that the trance-ecstatic religions annoyed Greek rationalists like Plato because they became *possession cults.*

> The Greeks had known four different kinds of trance: erotic trance, poetic trance, manic trance, and something Socrates called telestic trance. The last trance comes from the Greek word *telestai* meaning "ritual." Amidst frenzied dancing, which Plato in *The Republic* banned as "unfit for our citizens," the spirits of the cult came down and took up residence in the bodies of the dancers.
>
> —Rouget, p. 241

Rouget goes on to say that these were all surviving fragments of the ancient *goddess religions,* all of them *trance-possession cultures in which drums were probably the driving mechanism* (Ibid.).

Rhythmic Repetition

Most of the occult and hypnotic types of rhythms are repetitive, even monotonous. This is deliberate, for after more than one repetition of a rhythm the subconscious reaction tends toward anger and discomfort as the individual feels that the control of his feelings are slipping away and eventually, after many repetitions, individual consciousness is transferred over to group consciousness. After four repetitions of a particular rhythm the critical mind shuts down, allowing the subconscious to blend with other minds and the environment. *Spiritually, this is very dangerous because it leaves conscious control of your individual mind in the hands of others.*

Rhythm and Eselyn

From the '60s until now, the Eselyn Institute in Big Sur, California, was and is the "in" place to visit for New Age types looking for Eastern workshops on group consciousness, release from stress, tapping into the "collective subconscious" (a theory of Swiss psychiatrist Carl Gustav Jung), emotional therapy, and/or a general spiritual tune-up.

A favorite workshop is for tightly wound corporate executives. First they are flown into Monterey, California, and then taken by limousine to Big Sur, where they change into sweat pants and sweat shirt and are given a drum. All cell phones and other means of communicating with the outside world are confiscated. The rooms have no television, radio, or telephone. After they change into identical sweat pants and tops, they join a drum circle where a trained master drummer plays a particular rhythm and the uptight execs in their sweats join in by playing the same rhythm on their drum.

As one visitor described it, he could feel his individual identity slipping away, replaced by some sort of group consciousness. Although frightening at first, most found it very therapeutic. Psychologists tell us we all need to "get away" from ourselves, to detach ourselves from our critical left brain. Music is one way to do this, and repetitive rhythms are probably the fastest and simplest ways to accomplish this.

Today "drum circles" are showing up in grade schools, college campuses, and corporate executive retreats. Many are finding this a fun way to escape and enjoy the emphasis on the group rather than the individual, a form of music therapy.

Christian Rock Music

> Was there, immediately preceding Western "history," a drum-driven possession trance culture that worshiped the earth in the form of a Great Mother?
>
> —Hart, p. 207

In my book *All That Jazz: A History of Afro-American Music*, I discovered in my research of the tribal music of Africa, Polynesia, India, and other third world countries, including Tibet, that music was the *most essential part of these pagan ceremonies*. The primary purpose of the music was twofold: (1)

certain syncopated and repetitive rhythms *called up the spiritual deity* and (2) the repetitive sounds placed many in a state of semi or total hypnosis, thereby in many instances allowing the "demon" god to take over that person and use them as a "channeler" for supposedly "spiritual" messages.

> Working our way through the crowd and peering through the doorway we saw two Buddhist monks. One was *banging a brass plate*, while the other sat cross-legged in front of a small mound of red coals. The latter was a thirty-year-old medium that had been brought in to ascertain the source of the boy's physical problems. *We recognized him immediately as a weak-willed monk whose life was a revolving door for demonic spirits.*
>
> —George Otis, *The Twilight Labyrinth*, p. 26

Demonic Religions

> Was the near extinction of the drum from Western European culture due to the fact that the drum had been part of a possession trance culture that had been suppressed by its conquerors (the Indo-Europeans)?
>
> —Hart, p. 209

The sacred rhythms of many of these ancient demon-driven religions were brought to the New World by Negro slaves. In most instances, these rhythms combined with some basic Catholic theology (adoration of saints, etc.) and became *native religions* in Cuba (Santeria), Haiti (Vodun), and Brazil (Camobile and Macumba). These hybrid demonic religions are thriving, not only in the Caribbean and Latin America; they are now part of America's greater religious communities in expatriates from Cuba, Haiti, and Brazil. Many of these demonic-driven rhythms have drifted first into the jazz, blues, Latin, and now rock music. Today they are showing up on some of the recordings of the more paganized so-called Christian rock groups.

Warnings from Africa

> West African drum-driven religions preserved elements of the old goddess religion of the Neolithic. If this is true, then these rhythms are some of the most resilient on the planet. Five, ten, twenty thousand years—who knows how long they have been pulsing?
>
> —Hart, p. 223

African Christians and pastors immediately recognize these rhythms as spiritually *dangerous* and have issued warnings to their American brothers and sisters in the faith. Note the words of native Christian pastor Stephan Maphosa from Zimbabwe, Africa:

> I am very sensitive to rhythms in music for I was a drummer in my village before I became a Christian who participated in demon-calling ceremonies using rhythms. I have recently noticed in many of the so-called "Christian" music CDs given me by American missionaries and/or their children *the same beat or rhythms we used to call up our native gods.*
>
> —*www.evangelicoutreach.org*

In another instance, American pastor Joe Myers was visiting and fellowshipping with a group of native pastors in the Ivory Coast nation of Africa. He decided at one of their meetings to play some selections from his daughter's contemporary Christian CDs.

> There was an instant verbal and violent reaction. Angrily, these pastors took us to task by asking why we were allowing believers in the U.S.A. to "call up" evil spirits through *the native rhythms of tribal Africa*" (5:4).

Haitian Voodoo

> When the slave ships began plying the waters between the New World and West Africa (1612–1860), everyone thought they carried just strong, expendable bodies. *But they also carried the new counterculture—maybe even the (ancient) roots of the mother goddess culture—preserved in the form of drum rhythms that could call down the Orisha (tribal gods) from their time to ours.*
>
> —Hart, pp. 209–212

The driving drumbeats, bloody sacrifices, and hidden societies are rooted in the fertile religious soil of West Africa. At the time of Napoleon, Haiti was owned by France. There was a successful Negro slave uprising on the island around 1810. Distracted by major wars in Europe, France did not send enough troops to reverse the takeover. The African native who led the revolt openly boasted that he would turn the island over to the African "gods" if he was successful. Today Haiti, in spite of a potential strong economy in sugar cane and other crops, is one of the darkest spots in the Caribbean, and a representative Western democracy seems to have a difficult time finding roots on the island. Many superstitious people even today believe the island is cursed because of its dedication to dark spiritual forces.

Haiti and AIDS

In the first major book on the AIDS epidemic, *And the Band Played On*, the author mentions that Haiti was one of the most popular spots for male homosexuals to vacation because of the easy availability of nubile young boys. According to the book, a very sexually active male airline steward visited the island and contracted AIDS. He then spread it widely both inside and outside the U.S.A. because of his constant traveling and sexual proclivities. The book also suggests that the young boy who infected the airline steward was brought over from Africa, where the disease supposedly originated.

Vodun

Vodun is the French name for Haitian voodoo, which thrives on repetitive, loud, syncopated drumbeats, bloody sacrifices, and hidden societies . . . all practices that originated in West Africa. The guiding spirits of Vodun are called *loas* or *guides*. Originating in Africa, some of the names of the gods were changed, but the practice of using repetitive, syncopated drumbeats to call up foul, evil spirits is as ancient as Sodom and Gomorrah.

Cuba and Santeria

Catholic folk culture and ancient African demonic rituals joined forces on the island of Cuba in the form of a native religion called *Santeria*. In ethnic clubs known as *cabildos* or *reglas*, tribal drumbeats (on the male and female conga drum) announce the great festivals of Christian Epiphany: Carnival, Holy Week, and Corpus Christi. Members pour onto the streets of Havana (and now Miami) wearing masks of Yoruba (West Africa) tribal gods, while hosting icons of Catholic patron saints.

Santeria, or *the way of the saints*, is a highly ritualized occult religion ibining these two major influences. Devotees in training must wear pure white clothing. When you are in a Cuban community and you see someone dressed all in white, you can know that they are in training or one of the spiritual leaders of the local Santeria cult.

Native American Religions

There are many Native American religious rituals that involve ritual drumming to a specific beat, dancing, and demon possession. They too seek to call up "guiding" spirits. Today, tourists can visit the reservations of the Hopi and Navajo Indians in Arizona and at certain times of the year, witness these dances.

> Zuni Indians, for example, hold an annual *council of the fetishes* (a fetish is an everyday object that is given supernatural power through demonically-driven religion) in which gathered tribal fetishes are worshiped and energized by special night chants and offerings of prayer-meal.
>
> —George Otis, *The Twilight Labyrinth*, p. 10

According to Joseph Campbell, leading cultural anthropologist, the "shamans" or "medicine men" were probably the first spiritual leaders. Shamans were and are drummers. They are trance masters who have learned to use rhythm to create *altered states of consciousness* (Mickey Hart, *Drumming at the Edge of Magic*, p. 163).

Types of Trance

There are two types of drum-induced trance. The first is a possession trance. The spirits (called *loa* in Vodun) descend and invade the bodies of the dancers. The second type is a communion trance, where the spirit or soul of the drummer rides his drumbeat like a horse up to the spirit world where he (usually a male) transacts his business in an active rather than passive (prayer) way.

> —Ibid., p. 164

Dangers

There is a consistency to all the demon driven religions in the world. Their ceremonies all involve ritual drumming—usually highly syncopated patterns, often very loud. Dancing is often part of the ceremony. At some point, someone or several people's personalities "are taken over" (possessed) by dark forces. Often bloody rituals are included, as well as occasional sexual abandonment. *These same characteristics are today often found in our rock festivals and concerts, even among the so-called Christian rock groups.* When combined with the use of drugs or alcohol, the forces unleashed can be morally devastating.

Rhythm in Music in the Church

The early Christian church was well aware of the dangers of pagan, highly rhythmic, syncopated, sensual, loud, and repetitive drum-driven "religious" music. Even Christ warns His followers when praying (Matt. 6) not to "babble" like the heathens. As a result, church leaders for almost two thousand years have watched carefully to prevent these kinds of musical practices from sneaking into the church. As recently as the 1950s our culture realized and generally accepted that there were two basic musical styles: sacred and secular.

> With the adoption of Christianity by the Roman Empire percussive music was banned as "mischievous" and "licentious," the drum and cymbals were particularly singled out as evidence of the "devil's pomposity."
> —Hyslop, *The Two Babylons*, p. 175

Modern science has recently affirmed the reasons for resistance on the part of the church to highly syncopated music. The teachings of ancient India predate the recent scientific discoveries. In the Hindu discipline of Hatha yoga, it is taught that there are seven *chakras* or energy centers starting with the base of the spine and moving upward to the pineal gland, located between our eyes. Science confirmed these centers, only naming them as part of the endocrine system.

In Mickey Hart's book, *Drumming at the Edge of Magic*, he asks the question: "Why is noise that is produced by striking or shaking so widely used in order to communicate with the other [spirit] world?" (p. 114)

Mickey later discovered in an article, "A Physiological Explanation of

Unusual Behavior in Ceremonies Involving Drums" by psychologist Andrew Neher, his answer. Studying drumming in a laboratory setting, Neher found that he was able to "drive" or "entrain" the brainwaves of his experimental subjects down into what is called the *alpha/beta* border, which means that a majority of the electrical activity in their brains was pulsing at a rate of between six and eight cycles per second. The normal alpha/beta pulsation during activity is twelve to thirty cycles per second. This lowered pulsation is similar to the deceleration that takes place just before falling asleep.

Neher goes on to conjecture that percussion, particularly drumming, fulfilled the role of "driver" because drums *produced a sound that was so dense, so inharmonic, so fast-decaying and scattered across the frequency band that it overloaded the hearing mechanism. It was this overloading that helped induce trance.* (Ibid., p. 117)

Rhythm and the Endocrine Gland System

Besides activating the "fight-or-flight" response that is part of this system, loud, repetitious, syncopated rhythms can also stimulate the lower *chakras*, energy centers of the endocrine glands, particularly the gonads or ovaries— the reproductive glands.

Brain and Rhythm

Repetitive, syncopated, and loud rhythms can also lull the higher part of the brain into a state of hypnosis, allowing easier access to the mid-brain, the seat of our emotions. Madison Avenue, America's advertising center in New York City, realized early on that music was the most potent force in a radio or television ad. Unfortunately for advertisers, often the ads are too short to put the listener into a deeper state of hypnosis than they would like, so our logical higher brain can overrule our emotional mid-brain when we feel the urge to buy something as a result of the commercial that we really don't want or need.

Radio and television ad music is highly definitive of the types of music to trigger certain emotions, depending on the product. Lush, sensual rhythms for glamour products like clothes, shampoo, and perfume; aggressive, loud rhythms when selling autos or pick-up trucks; inspirational sounds when dealing with family values like houses, family cars, etc. *No one has spent more time and money on how to motivate the buying public through the use of music than today's advertising agencies.*

Black Churches

Even in the black churches raised on spirituals, gospel songs, and other Afro-American music, they still understood the difference between the "devil's" music and the music of the church. Beginning in the late 1950s, that barrier began to be broken down. Secular music not only joined forces with traditional sacred music, but in many mega-churches today secularized music has *replaced* two thousand years of sacred musical traditions.

If these were just social adjustments and changes, the problem would be minimal. However, the belief that you can write religious lyrics to a demonically driven rhythm and carnal musical presentation and have it be spiritually sanctified is naïve at best. The church has allowed Satan to slip into the sanctuary through these ancient musical practices that were at one time forbidden in the sanctuary.

As Mickey Hart explains on page 22 of his excellent book *Drumming at the Edge of Magic:* "These instruments [drums, percussion] are capable of releasing certain energies that you contact only when you play."

In a recent article, pastor and author *David Wilkerson (The Cross and the Switchblade)* closely monitored the penetration of liberal churches with contemporary so-called Christian rock music, and he claims that there has been a steady decline in moral sensitivity on the part of the young people and parishioners attending those churches since this trend. He sees Christian rock for the most part as demon-driven primitive occult-worship ceremonies repackaged with watered-down Christian dogma and words (CCM, Issue 7, 1997, "Charismatic Music Penetrates the Churches", p. 3)

Emotions and Rhythm

In the popular psychology book of the '70s, *I'm OK, You're OK,* Dr. Brendt identified what he called the four basic human emotions:

1. Mad
2. Sad
3. Glad
4. Scared

In my own research I would have to add:

5. Inspirational (religious, patriotic, brotherhood of man, ecological, etc.)
6. Humorous
7. Sensual

There you have it: seven basic human emotions balancing the seven parts of music. When you line up the correct musical formula in each of its categories to reinforce the emotion or emotions you wish to portray, you have the "magic" of music, and its foundation is *rhythm*.

What types of rhythms reinforce these emotions? Let's look at the following examples:

- **Mad:** Short, very jerky, exaggerated, syncopated rhythms; loud and unpredictable. Example: the famous shoot-out at the OK Corral in the Wild West beautifully captured in rhythm and sound by American composer Aaron Copland in his popular western ballet *Billy the Kid*.
- **Sad:** Slow, mostly even rhythms; little or no syncopation. Long note values. Example: "Somewhere" from Leonard Bernstein's popular Broadway musical *West Side Story*.
- **Glad:** Fast, running rhythms, slightly syncopated. Much repetition building to a big climax. Example: the bicycle-chase sequence from the Steven Spielberg film *ET*, music by John Williams, or the scene from the film *Titanic* where the romantically entwined are both on deck on the highest, most frontal position at the ship, letting the wind blow through their hair.
- **Scared:** Slow, winding rhythms with occasional sharp, unpredictable percussion sounds, often with an increasing pulse beat representing stress and fright. Example: Opening theme music from the scary Stephen Spielberg movie *Jaws*.
- **Inspirational:** Kate Smith singing Irving Berlin's "God Bless America," Woody Guthrie singing "Blowin' in the Wind," Civil rights protestors of the '60s singing "We Shall Overcome," or the "Battle Hymn of the Republic," played on the Fourth of July.

- **Humorous:** Henry Mancini's clever opening theme to the *Pink Panther* film with Peter Seller's as "Inspector Clouseau."
- **Sensual:** "Dance of the Seven Veils" music from the opera *Salome* by Richard Strauss, or the theme to the movie *Mambo Kings.*

The bottom line is that rhythm can enhance or even suggest strongly a particular emotion that the mind can and often does buy into. In other words, music can manipulate our moods, even without conscious approval. Like all powerful things in life, there's a good and bad side to all of this. On the downside, we are putty in the hands of Madison Avenue, who bombard us twenty-four hours a day with mass advertising on radio, television, and the movies. *We are being manipulated by rhythm and music whether we want to be or not.* The good side is that powerful rhythms can enhance drama, cinema, dance, and even sporting events.

Eurhythmics—New Science
A relatively new science has been created sometime within the past fifty years, the science and study of rhythm, hence *eurhythmics.* A scientific approach to the mysterious power of music, and in particular rhythm, has resulted in a whole host of breakthroughs in sports, work, public speaking, singing, and acting, as well as musical performance.

An enhanced rhythmic sense can improve our basic skills in one or more of the categories listed above. How do you enhance or strengthen your sense of rhythm? I thought you'd *never* ask!

Rhythmic skills are mainly enhanced through *moving to rhythm.* That's right, dance your way right into a more sensitive rhythmic sense! The contraction and relaxation of the large muscle groups of the body to rhythm strengthens our rhythmic sense. When I discovered this, I flashed back on an undergraduate college buddy who was a good pianist but had a lousy sense of rhythm. After studying tap dancing for less than a year, his rhythmic sense in his performances improved *dramatically.*

Move, clap, sing, or shout rhythms! Always tap your foot when playing or singing other rhythms! The measuring of one rhythm against the steady pulse of keeping time with your foot (or swaying your body, or moving your big toe inside your shoe, etc.) *dramatically* strengthens and improves your sense of rhythm.

Cultural Bias and Rhythm

How does a drum alter consciousness? Percussive sound or noise played loudly over time eventually overwhelms the hearing apparatus and this plays a large part in inducing trance, in a sense, "sensory overload."

Many believe Afro-Americans have a "natural" rhythm gene that is superior to that of Caucasians and other races. "Blacks have more rhythm!" has always been a common misperception. There is no gene for rhythm. Why then are they in most instances more sophisticated and superior in their rhythmic sensitivity? Primarily because in their subculture people *walked, ran, and danced to music more than the rest of society.* Other subcultures where rhythm is a strong element include Jews, Hispanics, and some Middle Eastern cultures. These cultures also seem to have a more highly developed rhythmic sense.

Finally, in discussing rhythm in association with the human brain, research at leading medical centers like the UCLA Medical Center in Los Angeles, California, tends to support the fact that the rhythmic skills involved in playing music tend to reside in the right hemisphere of the brain, the gestalt, spontaneous, emotional, and non-linear side. Hence, those with a strong sense of rhythm tend to be in most instances *right-brain* dominant.

Summary

Music, and in particular rhythm, is not emotionally or spiritually neutral. In fact, music is the language of emotions, and rhythm is the most powerful element. For almost two thousand years the Christian church has had a healthy respect for strong, loud, repetitive, syncopated rhythms and for the most part kept them out of the church, hence the division between sacred and secular music, a division which no longer exists.

Today's champions of loud Christian rock music in the sanctuary are on shaky ground. There is no *biblical, cultural, scientific, or logical reason* to introduce this sensuous, non-sacred music into the sanctuary. Proponents show an amazing arrogance, pride, and lack of sensitivity to older members of their congregations when they champion such dangerous changes in worship.

There is a type of music that ministers to and amplifies the carnal side of man. There is another, which nurtures and amplifies the Christian spiritual side of man. *Rock music has always been associated with the carnal and demonic (sex, drugs and rock 'n roll). It has no legitimate place in Christian life and ministry.*

> I know that it's possible to ride the rhythms of a drum until you fall into a
> state of receptivity that can be construed as the beginnings of trance.
>
> —Hart, p. 176

Rhythm is not only the most powerful element in music, it is the most dangerous. Underestimating the power of certain rhythms to override your conscious controls is just as naïve as believing you can drink a lot of liquor without feeling its effects. Properly and carefully used rhythm can inspire, elevate, relax, activate, and unify the listener. On the other hand, rhythm can be the catalyst that breaks down our cultural and religious barriers and takes us back to the primitive times, dangerous times.

We've already learned that music, and in particular the loud, repetitive, and syncopated rhythms used in much of our contemporary rock/pop music, can be a legal substitute for a dangerous mind altering drug. More care needs to be taken to protect our society from the spiritual, cultural, and moral degeneration found in contemporary music. Yes, there is a Pied Piper (the legend of Hamlin) that can lead our children out of the village and into darkness, but he doesn't play flute, *he plays drums.*

> There have been many times when I've felt as if the drum has carried me to
> an open door into another world.
>
> —Hart, p. 176

Rock Music

Rock music is intended to broaden the generation gap, alienate parents from their children and prepare young people for revolution.

—Paul Cantor, *Jefferson Airplane*

But they set their abominations in the house, which is called by my name, to defile it.

—Jeremiah 32:34

Around 1968, I was on my way to a meeting at Capitol Records in Hollywood, California. Screaming teenagers, mostly girls, surrounded the building. An armored Brinks truck was backed up to the back door of the building. Soon four young men dashed out, jumped in the armored van, and the van tore out of the parking lot with some teenagers trying to jump on.

I asked my companion, "What was that?" Her answer was that it was a new rock group from England called the *Beatles*. Capitol Records was their distributor, and they were there for a meeting. I said, "Oh, oh, here comes the British!" I was right. The *Beatles* and later the *Stones* went on to become two of the most popular rock groups of all time. The original, early Beatles looked cute and cuddly with their bangs (hair) and Little Lord Fauntleroy tailored clothes (neither lasted very long). However darker forces were at work in their road to success:

Help [early Beatles song] was made on pot. *A Hard Day's Night*—I was on pills. I've been on drugs since I was seventeen.

—John Lennon

Musical Nightmare

For there shall arise false Christs, and false prophets, and shall shew great

signs and wonders; insomuch that, if it were possible, they shall deceive
the very elect. Behold, I have told you before.

—Matthew 24:24–25

It's happening. We are being spiritually and morally deceived by allowing Christian rock to become part of our worship service. In fact, in some
churches today, it is the *most important part*, particularly if liberal pastors and
churches read and believe their own propaganda, that the "unsaved" will not
set foot in a church without it being filled with satanically-inspired music. It's
like a bad dream.

There are people on the dais in front of the church that look so spooky
I would call 9-1-1 if I saw them in my neighborhood: nose rings, tattoos,
dressed in black, purple and green hair, all with an attitude. This is worship?
These people, who I wouldn't let inside the front door of my house, are going
to lead worship? Have we lost our collective minds?

> I figured the only thing to do was to steal their kids. I still think it's the
> only thing to do. By saying that, I'm not talking about kidnapping. I'm just
> talking about changing young people's value systems which removes them
> from their parents' world effectively.
>
> —David Crosby, of Crosby, Still & Nash
> interview in *Rolling Stone*, Vol. 1

Rock music was a derivative of the earlier style of the '50s rock 'n roll. Rock
music was actually born in Europe and imported back into the U.S.A., even
though its roots were American. Rock music was group orientated, whereas
rock and roll elevated soloists as well as groups. Rock music was louder, an-
grier, more rebellious, and less "black" in its content and presentation. Rock
music was born in the 1960s and was the first of what could truly be called
an "international" style of pop youth music.

Pioneers

> What we dish out is the musical equivalent of war—war upon quiet, war
> upon dullness, war upon certainty and stability.
>
> —The Who, interview in *Rolling Stone*, Vol. 2

The major innovators and pioneers came mostly from Great Britain, with the *Beatles* and the *Rolling Stones* being the two strongest European forces in early rock music. The Stones are still performing, even though several are grandfathers today. The *Rolling Stones* began as a cover group for the cuddly *Beatles*. With a new manager they changed their persona and now set out to "free" teenagers from cultural restrictions and to irritate parents:

> Rock music is sex, and you have to hit them in the face with it!
> —Mick Jagger, *Rolling Stones*, taken from
> *The Satan-Seller* by Mike Warnke, 1972

Sex, Drugs and Rock

> If exposed long enough to the tom-toms [drums] and the singing, every one of our philosophers would end by capering and howling with the savages. . . . Assemble a mob of men and women previously conditioned by a daily reading of newspapers, treat them to amplified band music, bright lights . . . and in next to no time you can reduce them to a state of almost mindless subhumanity. *Never before have so few been in a position to make fools, maniacs, or criminals of so many.*
> —Aldous Huxley, *The Devils of Loudun*, 1952

The above was the battle cry of the culture rebellious hippies of the '60s. Today the musical style of rock and its billions of fans are just as closely tied to this motto as ever:

> "In rock, you're supposed to be outrageous," says Lou Cox, a New York-based psychologist who specializes in addictions. "Being bad is good. The culture is not only supportive of addiction," he continues, "it's as if there is a demand for it—like it's part of the *credibility package.*"
> —Michael Paoletta, *San Diego Union Tribune*, "Billboard 5/04"

Addictive?

The primary reason for the power and popularity of rock music is the fact that it can be addictive. I'm not talking just about "liking" the music, I am talking about a *physical addiction*. Rock music rediscovered the power of pagan music in its volume, repetitiveness, and highly syncopated rhythm patterns.

Loud rock music triggers the fight-or-flight response, initiates the first stages of hypnosis, and overcomes conscious resistance to becoming part of a group consciousness. Detoxing from rock music can be just as difficult as detoxing from cigarettes, alcohol, or so-called recreational drugs. In the chapter "By Their Fruits," you will see the struggle many in both the secular and so-called Christian rock community had to detox from this music.

Early Death

The average life expectancy of a full-fledged rock 'n roller is around forty years. So many of the greats checked out early: from Jim Morrison of the Doors, Keith Moon of the Who, Sid Vicious of the Sex Pistols, Jimi Hendrix, Janis Joplin, and Brian Jones of the Rolling Stones, to contemporary artists such as Bradley Nowell of Sublime, Shannon Hoon of Blind Melon, and Kurt Cobain of Nirvana.

There is a growing awareness that death is nature's way of telling you to slow down, as well as the economic reality that dead artists can't sell records . . . and benefit from it. Recent superstars like Whitney Houston, Courtney Love, Natalie Cole, Ozzy Osbourne, Mary J. Blige, Anthony Kiedis of the Red Hot Chili Peppers, Michael Jackson, and Dr. John represent just a partial list of those who have admitted addiction and have submitted to professional treatment.

> In the mid-1980s Aerosmith broke down the door that made it okay for big-name artists to go public with their sobriety, according to industry observers. In the years since, Eric Clapton, Boy George, Bonnie Raitt, James Taylor, Elton John, and others have all made their sobriety known.
> —Michael Paoletta, *San Diego Union Tribune*, "Billboard 5/04"

Is There Something in the Music?

> The loud sounds and the bright lights of today are tremendous indoctrination tools.
> —Frank Zappa, of Mothers of Invention, quoted from "Music in Education Today," by D. L. Cuddy, *Union Leader* (NH)

The fact that so many of the leading rock artists are addicted to drugs or alcohol or have died from overdoses, along with a very high percentage of their

fans, can't help but make one wonder if there is something in the music itself
that contributes to this plague.

> The big beat [rock] is deliberately aimed at exciting the listener. There is
> actually very little melody, only rhythm. . . . We seem to be reverting to
> savagery. . . . Youngsters who listen constantly to this sort of sound are
> thrust into turmoil. They are no longer relaxed, normal kids.
> —Dimitri Tiomkin, Academy Award-winning Hollywood film
> composer, quoted from "Music in Education Today," by D. L. Cuddy

I believe there is something in the music that contributes heavily to drug addiction. First, the volume itself, along with the sharp after-beat of the drummer, triggers the fight-or-flight response, causing the body to self-medicate
itself via the brain to the adrenal glands. Secondly, I believe the anarchistic
lyrics promote drug use, sexual promiscuity, and social rebellion. The costumes alone tell us that these are not normal human beings on stage.

Negative Physiological Effects
Dr. John Diamond, a New York City psychiatrist, studied rhythmic beats of
over twenty thousand recordings and concluded:

> A specific beat (stopped anapestic rhythm, which is contrary to our natu-
> ral body beats and rhythms) found in over half of the top hits of any given
> week *can actually weaken you. . . . It interferes with brain wave patterns, caus-
> ing mental stress.* Tests conducted in schools showed that students per-
> formed 15% better *without rock music.*
> —"Music in Education Today," by D. L. Cuddy

Study after study is increasingly showing the physiological and mental damage that can be self-inflicted on a teenager through rock music. Hearing loss
is a major complaint, and former President Bill Clinton, although still a relatively young man, had to be fitted for hearing aids five years ago. He blamed
his hearing loss on listening to loud rock music while growing up in Arkan-
sas.

How About the Brain?
The human brain is the most marvelous biocomputer ever invented. All

modern-day computers are modeled after the human brain. None have ever come close to duplicating its incredible abilities. However, the brain is delicate. Sudden, threatening changes in the environment (loud sounds), or dangerous chemicals (drugs, alcohol), or hypnotic stages can alter the brain permanently.

> *"Snapping"* depicts the way in which intense experience may affect fundamental information-processing capacities of the brain. The [negative] experience itself may . . . render the individual extremely vulnerable *to suggestion*. It may lead to changes that alter lifelong habits, values, and belief systems.
>
> —Flo Conway and Jim Siegelman: *America's Epidemic*
> *of Sudden Personality Change,* 1978

There is a popular teenage drug today called *Ecstasy*. It can actually burn holes in parts of the brain and destroy serotonin, the brain's natural chemical defense system for stress.

> It is now possible to get at a person, to convert and maintain him in a new belief by a whole variety of imposed stresses [that includes loud rock music] that end by *altering his brain function."*
> —*Battle for the Mind: A Physiology of Conversion and Brainwashing,* 1957

Troubled Teenagers

The second greatest cause of death among teenagers today is suicide (auto accidents are first). Studies reveal that most of these tragic early deaths were at least partially promoted by rock music and the use of drugs. There is a consistency here that is disturbing. Sooner or later, just as society had to get up the courage to challenge the tobacco industry, the concerned citizens of our society will have to challenge the powerful multibillion dollar a year recording industry and MTV.

> [Dave] Messina [rock star] says, "Today I'm in control of my drinking and addiction. But I'll be in recovery until the day I die."
>
> —Flo Conway and Jim Siegelman: *America's Epidemic*
> *of Sudden Personality Change,* 1978

Summary

Satan will go to any extreme to pollute the worship directed to the Lord so that it will be rejected. In this way he succeeds in hindering worship in spirit and in truth. He simply adds another spirit and mixes in a lie, knowing God will reject it. God must, and always does, reject *all worship that is not born of the Holy Spirit* and that is not all of truth. And even if that music inspires the performers and listeners, it does not get beyond the ceiling—*God won't touch it. He abhors it!*

—*Set the Trumpet to Thy Mouth*, David Wilkerson, 1986

Our Lord Jesus Christ reminds us several times in teachings and parables that only a good tree can bear good fruit. He told us to measure spiritual truth by the fruit it bears. Pasting the word "Christian" over a musical style based on everything that is base and vile in our culture—sex, drugs, rebellion, the occult, etc.—does not make it okay. Being popular with the kids does not make it okay. Bringing more people to church does not make it okay. *There can be no compromise with spiritual principles. Light can never surrender to darkness.*

I believe history will show that the big three—illicit sex, drugs, and rock and roll—contributed more to the destruction of the American Dream than any other cause. Our nation is rotting from the inside from the intrusion of evil into our entertainment centers. And now we want to bring it into our churches . . . I don't think so! I have yet to see one scripture that would indicate that rock music is appropriate for worship.

It is a false Jesus they are selling; it is a false form of worship they are producing; it is a false church they are building. They are at best the Laodicean church as described in Revelation 3: the final church before Christ's return—a worldly, wealthy, entertainment-mad, ego-driven, prideful church that Christ says is spiritually naked and blind. Christ promises punishment for this church. He also asks to be let back into the churches in His name that have so grieved the Holy Spirit the presence of Christ had to leave.

The Secret Message of "The Da Vinci Code"

Why this chapter in a book about Christian music? Because it is important to see that Satan is attacking Christ and the church through all the media: music, print, visual. My years of exploring the occult and my participation in Eastern religions and philosophies prior to my conversion, as well as my research on music, and in particular the demon-driven tribal religions of Africa, India, and Polynesia, qualify me to respond to the false teachings found in the widely popular book *The Da Vinci Code*.

Attack the Deity of Christ

From the beginning (Gen. 3) Satan has sought to both find and kill the Messiah or mock His claim of deity. All the aberrant forms of Christian religion start with the denial of the divinity of Christ. The Mormons believe Christ was Satan's twin brother; the Jehovah's Witnesses believe that Christ was a created being, an angel; the Christian Scientists believe in the "Christ consciousness; a metaphysical state that each of us can tap into."

The Da Vinci Code, Holy Blood, Holy Grail, The Koran, The Chronicles of Zion, The Gnostic Gospels, The "Lost" Books of the Bible, the "Lost" Books of the Bible Revealed, etc., all work very hard to remove Christ from being King of Kings and divine.

Genesis 3

Now the serpent [the shining one] was more subtil than any beast of the field which the LORD God had made. And he [the shining one] said unto the woman [Eve], *Yea, hath God said, Ye shall not eat of every tree of the garden?* And the woman said unto the serpent, *We may eat of the fruit of the trees of the garden: But of the fruit of the tree which is in the midst of the garden, God hath said, Ye shall not eat of it, neither shall ye touch it, lest ye die. And the serpent said unto the woman, Ye shall not surely die: For God doth know that in the day ye eat thereof, then your eyes shall be opened, and ye shall be as gods, knowing good and evil.*

—Genesis 3:1–5

Again, the devil taketh him [Jesus] up into an exceeding high mountain, and sheweth him all the kingdoms of the world, and the glory of them; And saith unto him, *All these things will I give thee, if thou wilt fall down and worship me.* Then saith Jesus unto him, *Get thee hence, Satan: for it is written, Thou shalt worship the Lord thy God, and him only shalt thou serve.*

—Matthew 4:8–10

[Jesus speaking to the Pharisees] *Ye are of your father the devil, and the lusts of your father ye will do. He was a murderer from the beginning, and abode not in the truth, because there is no truth in him. When he speaketh a lie, he speaketh of his own: for he is a liar, and the father of it.*

—John 8:44

Dan Brown has hit a home run with his wildly popular novel *The Da Vinci Code.* This is not his first venture into the occult world of secret societies and hidden agendas. Dan Brown's previous novel, *Angels and Demons,* dealt with the supersecret, supposedly world-dominating, organization called the "Illuminati."

What's going on? Well, for one thing the world is in a precarious quandary regarding its future. People want to know if and how we can escape the hurdles of weapons of mass destruction, worldwide terrorism, natural disasters, plagues, famines, etc. In other words, there is a *hunger* to know what's going on, who's running the show, and what is going to happen in the future.

There are only two sources for this kind of information: the Bible and occult literature. Both claim secret knowledge regarding the future of mankind. However, the Bible, one-third of which is prophetic—and more than two-thirds of those biblical prophecies have already been fulfilled—is the only *proven* reliable source for accurate futuristic prophecies.

Occult prophecies, such as those of Nostradamus, the Jewish Cabala (Babylonian magic mixed with Judaism), some Islamic and Buddhist prophecies, and supposedly "secret" knowledge about the destiny of mankind in organizations like the Masonic Order, the Lucis Trust, Theosophy, and general New Age literature are usually vague, contradictory and at best confusing.

Opposites

The universe is made up of opposites: up/down, hot/cold, fast/slow, etc. Should we be surprised to know that there is *good* and *evil* in the universe? Should we be startled to realize that there is a good, loving God who sent His son to die for us around two thousand years ago on a hill called Golgotha (the skull) in Jerusalem? Should we be surprised that there is a sworn enemy to God's plan, a fallen archangel originally called Lucifer (which means "light-bearer"), later to be called Satan (meaning "deceiver")? Why are we surprised to learn there are two plans for man's eternal soul: God's plan and Satan's plan?

God created the heavens and earth. Lucifer, once the highest angel in Heaven's hierarchy, decided to rebel and claim worship for himself instead of God and thus came up with an alternate plan for man's eternal destiny. This planned deception was launched *in the Garden of Eden* by the master deceiver, liar and murderer . . . and the plan is still active. In fact, Satan's plan for man's destiny is moving quickly toward a climax, hence the books, films, stories, secret cults, etc., devoted to publishing and pushing his plan forward are increasingly aggressive and active. These plans fall under the new and fastest-growing religion in the world, Secular Humanism, along with its more occult cousin, the New Age movement.

However, before Satan can cast his spell over those who do not belong to Jesus Christ, he first must discredit God's plan. What was God's plan?

For God so loved the world, that he gave his only begotten Son, that whosoever believeth in him should not perish, but have everlasting life.
—John 3:16

Satan must discredit, debunk, and destroy the concept of God's Son serving as a once-and-for-all sacrifice for the sins of mankind. As a result, we are increasingly seeing Bible "experts" attack (1) the virgin birth, (2) the divinity of Christ, (3) the promised return of Christ, (4) the "holiness" of God and His Son, (5) the spiritual war between the forces of good and evil, (6) the coming judgment for the unbeliever, and (7) the inflexible promise of God's plan that only through the acceptance of the sacrifice of God's Son on the cross can unregenerate mankind be redeemed; there is no other way:

> Jesus saith unto him, *I am the way, the truth, and the life: no man cometh unto the Father* [God], *but by me.*
>
> —John 14:6

According to Jesus and the Bible from beginning to end, there is only one way out of this life without having to endure eternal punishment for our sins, and that is through the blood and sacrifice of Jesus Christ . . . no other way! This means that Buddha, Lao Tse, Mohammed, Zoroaster, or any other real or imaginary religious leader *cannot* guarantee eternal salvation and forgiveness of sins.

Adolph Hitler's media genius, Joseph Goebbels, said the general public would eventually believe any lie, *if it were repeated over and over with conviction.* If Hitler was able to deceive an entire nation with his Third Reich, would it be impossible for a supernatural being like Satan to be able to eventually deceive most of mankind? Besides, unsaved mankind will do anything, believe anything, in order to get rid of the guilt that haunts them for ignoring the God that made them.

The Lies in the Da Vinci Code

One of Satan's favorite tricks is to mix truth with fiction. There has to be some truth in his deception to give credibility to the message. On the other hand, the lies are twisted in with truth in such a way that it seems impossible to separate them.

The provable mistruths in *The Da Vinci Code* include:

1. Jesus was not the Son of God, only a charismatic religious leader.
2. Jesus did not die on the cross, but survived, married Mary Magdalene, and raised a family.

3. When the Romans destroyed Jerusalem and the temple in A.D. 70, Mary and the children spawned by her supposed union with Jesus managed to escape to Europe, eventually settling in France and becoming part of the bloodline of future European monarchs. (What happened to Jesus?)

4. The false claim that the Bible is full of lies, mistruths, distortions, etc., through the insertions of false dogma by the early Catholic church over the centuries.

5. The excitement over the belief (based on this dogma) that at some point in the future, a world leader will emerge, sign a seven-year peace treaty with Israel, and also be accepted as the Jewish "Messiah" because of the Merovingian bloodlines supposedly going back to Mary Magdalene, Jesus, and their supposed offspring.

6. Nature religions, black magic, and the occult are the "real" religions of mankind and have been suppressed for political purposes by the church.

7. The Crusades were launched by the Catholic church to locate and seize any documents that proved that Jesus did marry Mary Magdalene and produce children.

8. The Knights Templar, guardians of the Temple Mount in Jerusalem during the Crusades, found such documents, secreted them to Europe, and used them to blackmail the church for centuries.

9. Most of the great European thinkers and artists from the fifteenth century on were members of secret societies that believed this story and that they hid in their writings, paintings, and music special codes that identified their beliefs.

10. The Holy Grail is a symbol for the womb of Mary Magdalene, who produced the progeny of Jesus . . . and that the *true* religion to come out of the Middle East at the time of Christ was really a goddess-based religion, supposedly suppressed by cruel and devious religious leaders.

The Bible

The Bible agrees with little of the so-called "truths" found or revealed in the *Da Vinci* book. However, the Bible does warn that in the final period just prior to the return of Christ there will be widespread and intense spiritual deception.

The Bible also agrees (Dan. 9:24–27; Matt. 24; 2 Thess. 2; Rev. 13) that at some point a world leader will emerge and claim to be the Jewish Messiah ... with supposedly authentic proof of his lineage. This world leader will not only deceive some of the Jews, but will deceive all except those who belong to Christ. He will eventually rule the world with a rod of iron, as well as lead the world into a catastrophic future climaxing in the Battle of Armageddon (Rev. 19). At this time, the Lord Jesus, the true Messiah, returns before mankind totally destroys itself (using Satan's suicidal plans) and casts this demon–controlled false messiah and his false prophet into the lake of fire for eternity.

Timely

The Da Vinci Code is timely, because it represents a first wave of satanic propaganda to convince unregenerate mankind that (1) Jesus was just a man, (2) there is no "Heaven" or "Hell," (3) there is no "savior" nor "devil," (4) there are many paths to "god", and most of them are okay, (5) the Bible is full of lies and deception, (6) sex and religion when combined are okay, and (7) a world leader will emerge from Europe (descended from the tribe of Dan) who will appear to be the "savior" of the world.

According to Scripture, and amplified by *The Da Vinci Code*, at some point the entire world, except for those who hold to the truths and accuracy of the Bible, will be deceived by this false plan and end up worshipping a fake messiah and accepting him as authentic.

The Da Vinci Code is not the first book or message regarding this coming charismatic leader. This knowledge has been hidden and guarded by secret societies for centuries. Why is it being revealed now? The fact that this secret knowledge is being revealed now to a worldwide audience can only mean that the biblically predicted spiritual and political deceiver is about to be revealed. If that is true, and it must be, for there could be no other reason to make this knowledge public, then we are closer to what the Bible calls the "end times" than we think.

Nothing New

There is nothing new under the sun. These dark forces, cults, and religious-sexual secret societies have been around since the fall of Adam and Eve. They prey on the uninformed, the innocent, those fascinated with evil, with promises of power, success, wealth, and those seeking sexual as well as perverted "religious" thrills.

Do you believe that God means what He says in the Bible? Do you believe that God puts up barriers to your "fun," "fulfillment," and "enlightenment" just to be a killjoy? Do you believe that God has hidden powerful supernatural truths from most of mankind, only to be revealed to the special few? Do you believe people are basically good and can achieve a happy afterlife by their own efforts? Do you believe that you will have a pleasant eternal afterlife without repenting of your sins and accepting Jesus Christ as your Savior? Do you believe sex outside of marriage, homosexuality, abortion, lying, cheating, even murder, are okay if you can justify it in your mind?

If you answered "yes" to any of the above questions, you are being deceived. Paul the apostle tells us in the Bible that Satan's favorite disguise is as an "angel of light." In the higher levels of the Masonic Order, the Illuminati, and the Lucis and Theosophist societies, their leader (Satan) is called an "angel of light." The essence of these false teachings is that Satan is the "good" guy and got it right in the Garden of Eden.

Satan's name before he rebelled before God and was thrown out of Heaven was Lucifer, which means "lightbearer." *The Da Vinci Code* and all these secret societies worship "the lightbearer." He is the one they are looking for to "save" the world. How wonderful it is to know that God, in His magnificent foreknowledge, *in scripture written thousands of years ago,* warned us of this coming spiritual deception!

The Accuracy of the Bible

The God of the Bible is real. The Bible is true. It is not filled with inaccuracies; it is the only dependable source for spiritual enlightenment and spiritual truth. Failure to obey its laws *always* results in death, pain, anguish, and suffering.

The very fact that the events and beliefs we read about in *The Da Vinci Code* were predicted in Scripture, along with serious warnings about the coming age of spiritual deception, should be enough for any truly reasonable man or woman to cast their vote for Jesus and the Bible, and turn to Him for protection and guidance during these difficult and confusing years.

The Bible is the only spiritual guide that has proven itself. The hundreds of fulfilled prophecies, the miracles in both the Old and the New Testament, the promise of eternal salvation for those who surrender to Christ, the promise of a bright, happy afterlife, and the promise of return when Jesus will judge the non-believers and clean up the ecological damage done to the earth, all those promises are based on solid support. What would be the point in rejecting these truths?

Historical Inaccuracies

There are many historical inaccuracies in The *Da Vinci Code*. It's a great adventure story, but the facts are few and far between.

1. There is no historical record of Jesus Christ surviving crucifixion and being spirited away from the tomb by His disciples. This false story, described in Matthew 28, was concocted by the Jewish high priest and the Jewish religious leaders of the time in collusion with the Roman governor, Pilate, to quiet and deceive the masses regarding the true nature and purpose of Christ's death and resurrection.

2. There is no historical evidence of Jesus marrying Mary Magdalene and producing children. By the way, if this was true, what happened to Jesus when Mary Magdalene fled to Europe with her children? The book is silent on this issue. If this account is true, what happened to Jesus? When did He die? How did He die? Where is He buried?

3. There is no definitive proof that the Merovingian line (the blood of Jesus and Mary Magdalene) would eventually mix with the royal bloodlines of Europe and would continue to this day.

4. There is no historical evidence that the Crusades were started to find these documents that would destroy Christianity as we know it. My research on the subject of the Crusades revealed that they were first started because Islamic militants were attacking Christians who were trying to visit the Holy Land on a pilgrimage, much as the Muslims do today in their *Haj*, their pilgrimage to Mecca. Can you imagine what would happen if we harassed and eventually prevented Muslims from visiting their most holy sites?

5. We do not know what (if anything) the Knights Templar brought back from the Temple Mount following the Crusades to Europe, but it is im-

portant to know that all meaningful documents related to Jews and their descendents were destroyed in the great fire and total destruction of Jerusalem and the Temple Mount by the legions of Titus for Rome in A.D. 70, almost one thousand years before the first Crusade.

6. Goddess religions have been around for a long time. They go back to Nimrod, Semiramis, and the Tower of Babel (Gen. 10–11). They usually are connected with ritualistic sex in some form or another. They are called "fertility" cults. They are dangerous to a society because they destroy the family unit, spread disease, confuse the bloodlines, and increase drug and alcohol use. They celebrate "the good old days" documented in Genesis 6, when prior to the flood the "gods" (Nephilim, fallen angels) came down from "heaven" and had sexual relations with earthly women, producing a race of giants.

7. Many of the historical figures the author claims belonged to these secret societies are incorrect. Isaac Newton was a born-again Christian. He was a good Bible scholar and was fascinated with the accuracy of Bible prophecy. Mozart dabbled with the Masonic Order in a desperate attempt find financial help for his projects, and he revealed some Masonic rituals in his German siengspeil, *Die Zauberflote* or *The Magic Flute*. Beethoven was incapable of maintaining normal social relationships, let alone those of a secret society. Napoleon was too egotistical to submit his will to any secret society, and Debussy was such a dreamer and nonconformist he could never be part of a disciplined secret cult.

8. The only truth that *The Da Vinci Code* and the Bible can agree upon are the many biblical prophecies that predict that at some point (and many believe this to be not too far in the distant future), a charismatic world leader will emerge from Europe, claim the Merovingian bloodline, be a descendent from the ancient Jewish tribe of Dan, and be accepted by some Jewish religious leaders as their messiah. This leader, Scripture tells us, will also rule the world with an iron hand for a very short period of time and will eventually bring total devastation to the planet (Rev. 6–19; Isa. 23–24; Zech. 12–14; Dan. 7–11).

Dangerous Books

The Da Vinci Code is a good "read," but for some who are spiritually naïve or ignorant of biblical and historical truths relative to the book, there is the danger of accepting the essence of the story as historical fact.

Recently the "Harry Potter" books opened up a can of worms concerning occult practices that can negatively affect and deceive our children regarding spiritual truths. *The Da Vinci Code* adds more confusion and spiritual deception, and lays the groundwork for Satan's masterpiece, the historical figure the Bible calls the Antichrist.

Summary

The fact that this story is coming out of the closet, so to speak, at this time is just another indication of the accuracy of Bible prophecy, because our Lord and Savior Jesus Christ Himself warned us clearly in His outline of events that will take place before His return in Matthew 24–25, Mark 13, and Luke 21. Jesus said the most common sign of the eminency of His return would be *spiritual deception.*

God challenges unregenerate mankind to prove Him wrong (Isa. 40–47). He dares Satan's followers to prove Him wrong, to prove that Jesus was not the Son of God, or that man can get to Heaven any other way than through the shed blood of our Lord and Savior Jesus Christ.

The Da Vinci Code is an answering salvo concerning the future of mankind to the incredible success of the "Left Behind" series by Tim LaHaye. Fortunately for us, the "Left Behind" series is based on solid biblical prophecies, while *The Da Vinci Code* echoes the same old lies Satan has kept trotting out for non-believers since the Garden of Eden.

Remember, Christ said that Satan was a liar, a deceiver, and a murderer (John 8). He's had thousands of years to practice spiritual deception. Also recall Paul's warning that Satan's favorite disguise is "an angel of light." Satan's deceptive plan regarding mankind worked in the Garden of Eden. Will it work today? Only if you choose to believe a lie and ignore the truth, which was given to us over a period of twenty-five hundred years by over forty authors . . . the spiritual truths found *only* in the *Holy Bible.*

Science and Music

A hippie at heart, Carlos Santana has long championed music as a potent force for creating positive vibrations that—as this veteran of the 1969 Woodstock festival puts it—*"can change your molecular structure."*
—George Varga, music critic, *San Diego Union Tribune*, May 30, 2004

We live in the age of science. There have been more scientific discoveries in the last one hundred years than in all the previous periods of history combined. Alvin Toffler, author of the popular book *Future Shock*, gives us this example. If you took the accumulated knowledge of mankind from ancient antiquity to the year 1900 and gave it a graph representation of one foot, then all the accumulated new knowledge from 1900 to 1950 would be *three feet high*. But here's the mind-blower: if you took all man's accumulated knowledge from 1950 to the present it would be (in comparison) *taller than the Washington Monument*.

Music Research

Recent discoveries in music therapy research have been startling. Some of them hearken back to more ancient times, when the early Egyptian and Greek civilizations used music therapeutically for physical and mental healing. In addition to the positive discoveries being made, some disturbing discoveries have been made as well.

Certain styles of music can make you sick—mentally and/or physically. Music can put you into an "altered state of consciousness" (without you knowing it). Music can calm or enrage you. And music can be used as a habit-forming drug.

Below are some of the more startling discoveries regarding music. It's important to know that the human body is in a constant state of homeostasis, trying to adapt to changes in our environment. This has been one of the reasons we have survived; man can adapt to almost any environment, given the chance. For instance studies have shown that low-frequency sound pulses (usually from the electric bass) that are near our heart rate zone (seventy-two beats per minute at rest) will cause our bodily system to *lock on* to the bass beat. Video game musical soundtracks that start slow, then accelerate are *the most popular* (Branco Costello, M.D., Acoustic Clinic, Lisbon, Portugal).

Music affects positively and/or negatively this defense mechanism. Also, music because it is vibration, penetrates the body, affecting the nervous system, the five senses, the internal organs, the endocrine system, and other lesser-known but necessary systems for our complex body to grow, be healthy, and be effective. Again, recent studies have revealed that music affects our subconscious life support systems, like our circulatory, digestive, glandular, and other vital support systems of the body.

> Music can lower blood pressure, adjust our basal-metabolism, effect our respiratory rates [lessens or increases stress, depending on the style of music], can increase the bodies production of natural endorphins [pain relievers], speed healing, reduce the danger of infections and balance or imbalance [again, depending on the style of the music] the right and left hemispheres [cerebral cortex] of the brain.
> —*Reader's Digest*, "Music's Surprising Power to Heal," August 1992

Music Can Heal

"Music reduces staff tension in the operating room," says Dr. Clyde L. Nash, Jr., "and also helps relax the patient." (He uses classical music such as Vivaldi and Mozart.)

> —*Reader's Digest*, August 1992

More and more doctor's are exploring the ability of music to aid the medical process, particularly in the area of healing. Some dentists are experimenting with music instead of anesthetics for small local dental surgeries. Some doctors are using music as a replacement for harsher mood-controlling substances:

"Half an hour of music produced the same effect as ten milligrams of Valium," says Dr. Raymond Bahr, head of the coronary-care unit.(ibid)

—*Reader's Digest*, August 1992

Some studies show music can lower blood pressure, basal-metabolism, and respiration rates, thus lessening physiological responses to stress. Music may help increase production of endorphins and S-IgA (salivary immunoglobulin A) which speeds healing, reduces the danger of infections, and controls the heart rate. Studies indicate that both hemispheres of the brain are involved in processing music. Dr. Sacks explains "the neurological basis of musical responses is robust and may even survive damage to both hemispheres" (*Reader's Digest*, August 1992).

Can Music Harm?

An American high school student, David Merrell, was so convinced that *hard rock music* is bad for the brain that he picked up seventy-two male lab mice, a stopwatch, a 5′ x 3′ maze, and some CDs to prove his point. David said a group of mice exposed to hard rock music took thirty minutes to bump through his maze. The same mice had gone through the maze in ten minutes just three weeks earlier, before being exposed to rock music. "It was like the music dulled their senses, " David said. "It shows point-blank that hard rock has a negative effect all around."

David's experiment included three groups of twenty-four mice: a control group (no music), a hard rock group, and a classical music group. The mice spent the first week getting adjusted to David's basement. They received measured feedings and twelve hours of light daily. Each mouse navigated the maze to establish a base time of about ten minutes. David started playing music ten hours a day. The control group navigated without music. He put each mouse through the maze three times a week for three weeks. The results are startling:

"The control group cut *five minutes* from its original time. The mice that listened to Mozart knocked *eight and a half minutes off their time*. The hard rock mice didn't even bother to sniff the air to find the trails of the other mice and *lost 20 minutes*."

David learned to house each mouse in separate quarters. In a previous experiment the preceding year, he housed each group together: "I had to cut my project short because all the hard rock mice *killed each other*," David said. "None of the classical mice or control group did that at all" (Associated Press, February 12, 1995).

Recently, research on operating an automobile while listening to loud rock music revealed that the music somehow slows the reaction time of the driver (University of Sydney, Australia)

Sound as a Weapon

According to the March 8, 2004, edition of the *LA Times*, some rotating troops to Iraq are being trained and issued a new sonic weapon, one that looks like a small satellite dish. The user points the dish toward an unruly or threatening crowd of Iraqis and turns on the sound. A message in Arabic is given to disperse, followed by a shrill, sharp sound that is so uncomfortable that all but the most pain-resistant leave the area immediately. The pain, according to researchers, is not unlike "the mother of all migraine headaches." Naturally the troops are protected from the adverse effects of this device.

Law enforcement as well as the Pentagon has been looking for a long time for a safer, more modern way of dealing with riots and unruly gatherings. This new sonic weapon may be part of the answer.

Another new sonic weapon produced by the American Technology Group, San Diego, California, is the *Sonic Pain Stick*. It is excellent for crowd control in small spaces, and possibly even to foil airplane hijackers. When aimed at the culprit, it emits a shrill, high-frequency sound within a small radius that can drop anyone to their knees in intense pain.

Music Can Kill

In the recently popular science-fiction movie *Minority Report*, Tom Cruise introduces a new weapon. The gun is a sound wave gun that can be set to stun or kill. Unlike the rest of the story, which is set in the future, such a weapon exists today and is being tested by our military and law enforcement (*Village Voice*, April 12, 2004). The U.S. government has perfected a weapon using low-frequency sound waves. These new and supersecret weapons are called *acoustic* or *sonic* weapons. (See *U.S. News & World Report*, July 1997.)

Sonic weapons can vibrate the insides of humans to stun them, nauseate them, or even "liquify their bowels and reduce them to quivering diarrheic messes," according to a Pentagon briefing. Electromagnetic waves are being used to put to sleep or to heat up [microwave] an enemy. Scientists are experimenting with a sonic cannon that throws a shockwave with enough force to *knock down a man.*

Sudden bursts of extremely high volume (90 decibels and above) can (1) temporarily destroy hearing, (2) cause mental confusion and disorientation, (3) breakdown resistance to interrogation, (4) cause "tinnitus," a painful condition that usually manifests with a loud ringing or buzzing of the ears.

The research of French scientist Vladimir Gavreau in this field has revealed some startling discoveries: extremely low-frequency vibrations can make a potential enemy ill or even *kill* them under certain circumstances (*The Sonic Weapon of Vladimir Gavreau,* by Gerr Vassilatos, *www.border-lands.com/archives/arch/gavreaus.htm*). The *range of death* was found to lie between *three and seven cycles per second.* Sounds this low cannot be heard by the human ear, although certain animals, including elephants, communicate via low-frequency sound.

A few seconds of exposure to these dangerous sonic sounds create symptoms that come on rapidly and unexpectedly. Their pressure waves impacted against the *entire body* in a terrible and inescapable grip. The grip was a pressure which came in on one from all sides simultaneously, an envelope of death. Next came the pain, dull infrasonic pressure against the eyes and ears. Finally the low-frequency pressure waves begin to impact the environment, causing rooms and buildings to shake like an earthquake (ibid, p. 4).

The physical symptoms lasted *for hours* after the sound generators were turned off. Eyesight can be affected for days. Internal organs—the heart, the lungs, stomach, intestinal cavity—were filled with continual painful spasms for an equal time period. According to the scientists engaged in this research, if the sound had not been turned off quickly all the resonant body cavities that absorbed this low-frequency acoustic energy would have been torn apart.

Physiology seems to remain paralyzed by infrasound. It causes middle ear disruptions resulting in dizziness and nausea. Complete restoration can take hours or even days. Prolonged exposure can result in death. Symptoms increase in severity as the frequencies diminish, beginning with one hundred, which is still in the pre-lethal level.

Lethal infrasonic pitch lies in the seven-cyle range. Intellectual activity is inhibited, blocked and *then destroyed*. The action of the medulla is physiologically blocked, its autonomic functions cease.

The earth acts as a conduit for these low-frequency sounds, allowing them to travel long distances without diminishing their impact. They cannot be located by a potential enemy without special detecting devices.

Robotic tanks equipped with infrasonic generators could sweep an area with deadly infrasound, destroying all enemies within five miles. Drone jets could be used to destroy an approaching enemy. A sobering thought is the fact that as of now, *there is no foolproof defense for this system*.

On a less threatening level is the development of a new science called *hypersonic sound* (*www.khouse.org/6640/prophetic/BPO50.html*)._Developed by Woody Norris of *American Technology*, it's definitely the new wave of the future in audio technology. HSS waves can be directed at a specific individual or group. They are encased in the HSS soundbeam. *Only those in the soundbeam can hear the beamed music or message.*

It's been likened to a flashlight beam that can only illuminate the area within the beam. At 30,000 cycles the sound quality is so real that the listener feels as if the sound is being generated *within his head*. This beam can travel up to 160 years without any distortion or loss of volume. On the military side, if the volume is advanced to 145 decibels, or 50 times beyond the human threshold of pain, a burst of HSS sound could *destroy an enemy* and confuse it by bouncing the sound off walls, buildings, etc., making the sound seem like it is coming from many different directions (*Newsweek*, "Hearing Is Believing," August 5, 2002)

An experimental police whistle of 1.3 meters in diameter produced an infrasonic pitch of *37 cycles per second*. The sound that was produced violently shook the walls of the entire laboratory complex, even though its intensity was less than two watts (ibid, p. 3).

Nicholas Tesla, an eccentric Romanian-American scientist, was a contemporary of Thomas Edison. In fact, Tesla claims Edison stole his invention of the incandescent light bulb and passed it off as his own. A brilliant eccentric, he was ahead of his time in many ways. One of these ways was his research with sound. Tesla nearly destroyed his laboratory on Houston Street with his experiments on infrasonic impulsers.

He later tested infrasonic impulse weapons capable of wrecking buildings and whole cities on command. He artificially produced a small earthquake in Colorado Springs, Colorado, with one of his experiments in the early 1940s. Tesla died in the 1940s, while living in obscurity in New York City. Before the FBI could get to his apartment, the Russian KGB had already been there and confiscated the notes governing his research over the years.

Rock Music and General Health

We can see, then, that music affects the body in two distinct ways: directly, as the effect of sound upon the cells and organs, and indirectly, by affecting the emotions, which then in turn influence numerous bodily processes.

—David Thane, *The Secret Power of Music*, p. 137

As revealed by the opening statement, music affects our bodies and the cells of our bodies, first of all through the penetration of our bodies and cells by the vibrations (and volume) of the music and, secondly, through the emotional changes that cause the brain to send signals to various systems of the body to speed up, slow down, secrete a particular hormone, or shut down. As mentioned earlier in the book, man is constantly in a state of *homeostasis*, an attempt to adjust physically, mentally, and emotionally to changes in our environment.

Increasing studies are showing that rock music can be dangerous to our mental, emotional, and physical health, besides wreaking havoc with the moral base of civilization with its battle cry of "sex, drugs and rock 'n roll." I believe that listening to too much rock music at too loud a level is *more dangerous* than cigarette smoking, because it affects other systems of the body as well. I hope that we are in the early stages of realization regarding this danger, as we were with cigarette smoking twenty years ago . . . truth has a habit of not going away or staying buried.

Julius Portnoy (a leading scientific musicologist) as found that not only can music "change metabolism, affect muscular energy, raise or lower blood pressure, and influence digestion, but it may be able to do these things more successfully . . . *than any other stimulants that produce these changes in our bodies.*" (Ibid, p. 138)

I Think I'm Going Out of My Head

> To maintain a sense of well-being and integration, it is essential that man
> is not subject too much to any rhythms *not in accord with his natural bodily*
> *rhythms.*
>
> —David Thane, *The Secret Power of Music,* p. 199

The sharp backbeat (soft/loud) of the drummer in rock music is the *antithesis* of the natural rhythm of the heart (loud/soft). The automatic nervous system will try to adapt (homeostasis) to its most immediate aural, visual, and physical environment. The reverse pattern of the natural heart rhythm can cause heart arrhythmia and other cardiac problems if prolonged, or if the person has a heart problem to begin with. This might explain the rash of young people dying of heart attacks at ages way below the normal for that type of physical degeneration.

Do You Hear What I Hear?

Audiologist Kathleen Bulley tests and evaluates hearing at Scripps Hospital in La Jolla, California. She has noticed an increase in young adults coming forward with hearing loss.

> Whether there really are more with hearing loss is hard to say. Actually,
> when President Clinton admitted he had a hearing problem [he also likes
> to listen to loud rock music; read the new book *Air Force One*] and not
> being an elderly president—it inspired a lot of people in their 30s and 40s
> to come forward.

Bulley says there is a *real danger* to listening to loud music, especially in an enclosed area like a car (or a church).

> When people expose themselves to excessive noise levels, the ear is being
> bombarded with the pressure of the sound and, depending on how long
> they're exposed, the volume level of the sound, it can result in a temporary
> hearing loss. It usually starts out in the high-frequency range—like how
> your ears feel stuffed after a loud concert.

To show specifically how hearing loss can be incurred by listening to loud music, Bulley cites OSHA guidelines for noise exposure.

> This is their criteria, but it is a governmental guideline. It can vary because people are individuals. For example, it says that 90 decibels for eight hours can cause permanent hearing loss. It drops pretty fast after that: at 100 decibels, it's two hours. At 105 decibels, one hour. At 110, thirty minutes. At 115, fifteen minutes.

What does this mean for the people McCullough mentioned who regularly listen to 160 decibels or more?

> The hearing may not go on one exposure. Did he really say 200 decibels? Because at 180, *people start feeling like they are coming apart!*

No Neutral Ground

> Like human nature itself, music cannot possibly be neutral in its spiritual direction . . . . Ultimately all uses of tone and lyrics in music can be classified according to their spiritual direction, upward or downward. To put it plainly, *music tends to be of either the darkness or of the light.*
> —David Thane, *The Secret Power of Music*, p. 187

Fans of loud, syncopated, repetitious music, often with salacious or anarchistic lyrics, claim that all art, including music is "amoral"—without moral intent; innocent of any "feelings" except those projected on it by the listener. There is no logical, moral, or scientific support for such a statement, yet it is made to justify the evil and health-damaging music sold in this country to the tune of $15 billion a year . . . more than the profits from cinema, live concerts, and professional sports combined (*San Diego Reader*, "Calendar/Music Scene," p. 9, April 18, 2001).

"By their fruits ye shall know them"

Testimonies of Repentant Christian Rock Devotees

Rock Music Is Addictive

Until I began my research for my book *All That Jazz: A History of Afro-American Music*, I would have laughed if someone had suggested that certain styles of music could be addictive. I believed that being "hooked" on a certain style of music was only a stylistic preference. Boy, was I wrong!

Further research on my first book in this series, *Crisis in Christian Music* (available through Southwest Radio Church, 1-800-652-1144) opened the door to the primary reasons for the power of rock music. *Rock music can be physically and emotionally addictive.* I qualify this statement in this book with solid research that proves this point. *Rock music is a drug.* The volume, repetitiveness, syncopated rhythms—all combine to trigger certain chemical changes in the body that gives the listener an incredible high.

Hiding these facts behind religious lyrics does not change the result. The struggle to free oneself from this addiction is a real one, as many of the unsolicited testimonies given below illustrate. Eager pastors wanting to fill their pews to overflowing give the kids the music they want. They rationalize away the reasons for more mature believers fleeing their churches. They have not only unleashed Satan in the sanctuary, but they have unknowingly "hooked" many people on rock music. God will hold them responsible for this.

Love Not the World

How a mature Christian could ever believe that good fruit could come from a sin-ridden source is beyond me. The desire for recognition, fame, integration with the power brokers of the world, and unbelievable pride and arrogance have all gone into unleashing a force that is not only leading congregations astray, it is inducing many into an addiction they enjoy, or, if they see through the satanic trap, have a difficult time detoxing themselves from. That's why I have titled both these books *Crisis in Christian Music, volumes 1 and 2 . . . we are in a crisis regarding the deadly deception let loose upon us within the church.*

The Struggle

The following are unsolicited testimonies of repentant, mostly young Christians who were able to eventually see through the deception of Christian rock music and turn from it, returning to true, sanctified worship, uncontaminated by the world or the forces of darkness. Many thanks to *www.av1611.org* for their permission to reprint some of these testimonies, as well as others I have received from those who read my first book, *Crisis in Christian Music,* and realized that they had been deceived. Note: There are some spelling and grammatical errors in the testimonies below. We print them as we received them. The emphasized text is editorial.

◆   ◆   ◆

I was following the Lord wholeheartedly until we switched churches and I was invited to the new youth group. I had a conviction against rock music, but as I was surrounded by it, my beliefs were corrupted. This music eventually led to rebellion and moral failures. The Lord has gained a victory in my life now, but the music still brings on rebellion if I listen to it. *Please get rid of this music and play melodious harmonious music!*

—A 15-year-old student from Pennsylvania

◆   ◆   ◆

"Christian rock" had made me a shallow, rebellious young Christian. It made it easy for me to get into regular rock music. When I finally submitted to God and got the rock music out of my life, *I was able to see the double standard that is lived out by "Christian rock" musicians. "Christian rock" does not praise God and it is worse than regular rock because I think it is hypocritical.* Rock is wrong and addictive and has contributed to my moral failure. I praise God for His help in releasing me from it.

—An 18-year-old student from Indiana

◆   ◆   ◆

I began to listen to "Christian rock" without the blessing of my father. He told me that if I listened to "Christian rock" it would open the door for Satan. I just laughed and listened anyway. *It totally deadened my Christian growth* and led to terrible immorality, rebellion, and rejection of God. It then developed into secular hard rock. Now all I can do is go back and pick up the pieces. *But I still have a scar in my life that will never be removed.*

—A 16-year-old student from Oklahoma

◆   ◆   ◆

"Christian rock" has hindered my life because the only difference between "Christian rock" and secular rock *is the words.* The beat, rhythm, and the melody are not different; they are the same.

—A 21-year-old student from Michigan

◆   ◆   ◆

Christian rock at one time really messed up my view of Christianity. I would listen to it and think, "Look how Christianity is trying to blend in with the world." . . . I have totally avoided this music and have considered it ungodly and unscriptural!

—A 19-year-old student from Ohio

◆   ◆   ◆

Christian rock was a big part of my life about six months ago. It totally consumed me. *I lived in the bondage of this music* and the bondage of the music of my friends' preference, which was not very good either, to say the least. I realized that this ungodly music *did not glorify God and never will.*

The main things I learned this week [summer Bible camp] are that we as Christians do not take drugs to witness to drug users, and we do not convert to worldly habits to identify with the world. *I saw no reason to use worldly music with Christian words so that I could minister to the world!*

—A 17-year-old student from California

◆   ◆   ◆

When I got started listening to contemporary Christian music, I started out on "mild" music, but it grew to harder music. *It grew to the point where the music took the place of Bible reading.* . . . It was addictive, and I held some back. Later, it was brought to my attention that when you cannot get rid of something in your life that keeps you from God *it is an idol.* This music, which is supposed to promote Christianity, caused me to violate God's commandments about idolatry.

—A 17-year-old student from Missouri

◆   ◆   ◆

When I began listening to "Christian rock" my personal devotions were almost nonexistent. *"Christian rock" deafened my Christian "immune system"* (conscience) *to rock music.* When I listened to this music, I would fall away from and rebel against my parents. "Christian rock," in my opinion, distorts hymn. I can remember a "Christian rock" beat to most of the hymns I have sung. *I strongly encourage not getting into this music.*

—A 17-year-old student from Missouri

◆   ◆   ◆

"Christian rock" has damaged my life in two ways. First, it ruined my Christian witness. The addictive beat and tempo were very hard for me to conquer. When I went to a friends house, instead of being two friends together talking we would sit in his room and do nothing except allow the music to flow through us. Second, the beat and words are still a part of my life. Many times as I was listening to "Christian rock," my mind would go to the words of secular rock. Even now, after destroying all this wrong music and committing myself to God's music, I still have a rebellious attitude well up inside me. "This will be a very hard habit to break."

—A 16-year-old student from Michigan

◆   ◆   ◆

"Christian rock" music has divided my youth group. It has kept me in bondage spiritually, and my relationship with my sister has been deeply hurt. I see the rebellion in both of us after we are exposed to rock. *Whenever I walk into my youth group, rock is being played. I feel Satan's control start to tighten.* One of my closest friends has remarked about the difference in my countenance after I have listened to this music. I find it almost impossible to have a beneficial, reverent quiet time when the sensual beat pops into my mind.

—A 17-year-old student from Georgia

◆   ◆   ◆

I listened to rock music for about four years and it was not "Christian rock" because *I always thought it was so hypocritical to listen to Christian rock.* At least I was honest about it and I did not pretend to be somebody I wasn't. So, after the first couple of times I was already addicted to it. The reason I started is because everybody always thought I was a "goody-goody." The would say, "Hey, did you hear that song?" or "Have you ever heard this group?" I would say, "No, I listen to rock." I began by listening to "soft rock" and progressed to heavy metal. It really had a strong effect on my life. *Now my church plays "Christian rock" and I see it ruining many kids in our youth group. It is so sad. It has ruined kids that were so sweet."*

—A 16-year-old from Texas

In Closing

I have selected just a few of hundreds of testimonies pouring into anti-Christian rock media outlets and pastors who have had the courage to stand up and drum the devil's music out of their church. There is a growing realization among young Christians that *there is something wrong, something spiritually not sound, about Christian rock music.* You will notice a pattern in these repentant confessions:

1. How "easy" it is to slip into Christian rock music.
2. How addictive the music is.
3. How there is a desire to explore secular rock as well.

4. How it contributes to a spirit of rebellion.

5. How it ruins a Christian witness.

6. How it leaves the addict spiritually frustrated and frightened.

7. *How few refer to any recorded example or artist* or song as being okay.

8. How it has a negative effect on their relationship with their parents.

9. How the music contributed to immoral behavior.

10. How compromise doesn't work; the music eats up your hours, your days.

How much longer are we going to stand by and watch our children being led away by the modern Pied Piper of Hamlin: rock, Christian rock, MTV, VH1, etc? When and where are we going to draw the line? My wife and I have been in churches recently where we feel more like having a scotch and a cigarette then preparing ourselves for worship. *It's time for the body of Christ, for those that really love the Lord, know their Bible, and recognize these signs as signals of the eventual return of Jesus Christ, to choose. Choose whom you would serve. The Bible tells us to "come out" of carnal churches, ministries.*

Evangelism via Christian Rock

Most of the Christian rock groups rationalize their performances as evangelical outreaches. First of all, in most instances, the words are barely intelligible because of the volume and distortion. People do not sing in rock music; they shout, they scream, they growl, they moan. Secondly the costumes, the arrogant stage presence, all are imitations of secular rock groups. Third, the plan of salvation is never made clear, people are not made aware of their sinful nature, and there is seldom if ever an altar call. Fourth, the groups themselves are more concerned about making it in the secular Christian rock music field then witnessing. Fifth, in most instances the lives of the individual performers leave a lot to be desired as role models for a newly redeemed Christian.

Increasingly, Christian rock groups are appearing on the same stage with secular rock groups, many of whom spew out filth and vulgarity at ear-splitting levels before or after the Christian rock group plays. *There is no reason for this mixed bag of so-called sacred and secular except to pursue worldly lusts of wealth and fame.*

The San Diego Fair is the eighth largest in the nation. It's a big deal. It begins in mid-June and runs past July 4. To appear on the big stage at night is a large step for an up-and-coming music group. Recently a local "Christian heavy-metal" rock band were invited to play at the fair. In the newspaper interview prior to their appearance—an opportunity to witness to the press about Jesus and their "evangelical" fervor—*nothing was said. Jesus' name was never mentioned.* However, the possible commercial future of this group was discussed at length. Some quotes from the article include:

1. "MxPx finds subjects beyond chicks, cars and beer for a punk tune, providing self-realized soul searching in the band's lyrics" (reporter).
2. "I guess the way I try and incorporate my personal beliefs in the music is just being honest with myself; writing about things I feel and writing about things I care about" (bass and lead singer Mike Herrera).
3. "In that way, I'm reflecting who I am as a person, but at the same time, *I'm not here to tell people what they should believe*" (Mike Herrera).

—San Diego Union Tribune, June 24, 2004, music section, p. 19

These young musicians could have been Buddhists, Muslims, atheists, or any other religion or cult in the world. There was no way to connect them to Christ. How sad. How dangerous to use the exalted name of God's Son, Jesus Christ, to get a leg up on fame and fortune. In Matthew 7—the end of the Sermon on the Mount—Christ addresses future "devotees" who preach, witness, heal, and I suppose sing in His name, but for false, selfish, fleshly reasons. Christ's words are strong: ***"Begone, I never knew you!"***

Quo Vadis?

Quo Vadis is Latin for "which way are you going?" There is a legend that when severe persecution of the early Christian church broke out in Rome (Nero blamed the Christians for the fire that destroyed over half of the city) around A.D. 65, that the apostle Peter, who was in Rome at the time, fled the city. According to this legend, at the top of hill overlooking the Seven Hills of Rome on the Appian Way, Peter saw His Lord, Jesus Christ, walking toward him. Peter asked His Lord: *"Quo vadis?"* "Which way are you going?" Christ supposedly replied, "To Rome, to die [once again] in your place." Peter, realizing that fear had almost caused him to deny his Lord again, broke into tears and pleaded with his Lord not to do this, turned around, and headed back to certain death.

According to legend, Peter was crucified upside down (at his request, as he felt he was not worthy to die in the same manner as Jesus) on a small hill you can still see today as you look out of one of the upstairs windows of the Vatican Museum. Holy Scripture tells us that it is a distinct honor to suffer and in some cases die for our faith and for our Lord. Today many are dying for their faith in places like the Sudan, China, Iran, Saudi Arabia, the Philippines, Indonesia, and Africa. Do we want to corrupt these noble sacrifices by allowing the world into the church through its music rather than taking the church out into the world?

Courage

Revelation 21 lists the characteristics of those who will be denied admittance to the New Jerusalem and the New Heaven and Earth:

> He that overcometh shall inherit all things; and I will be his God, and he shall be my son. But the fearful, and unbelieving, and the abominable,

and murderers, and whoremongers, and sorcerers [*pharmacia*=drugs], and idolaters, and all liars, shall have their part in the lake which burneth with fire and brimstone: which is the second death.

—Revelation 21:7–8

Note that "courage" is at the top of the list of qualifications to get into God's new home. Most of us who live in the United States are not used to having to stand and defend the faith or suffer persecution for our beliefs. Those times are coming; those times are here. Taking a stand on the importance of spiritually conceived music for worship is important, even if it costs you friends, employment, or the need to drop out of a church you have long supported.

Apostasy

Apostasy: *a deliberate repudiation and abandonment of the faith that one has professed* (Heb. 3:12). "Wait a minute," cries the Christian rock church, "we haven't abandoned the faith!" Christ's answer to that is found at the end of the Sermon on the Mount:

Not every one that saith unto me, Lord, Lord, shall enter into the kingdom of heaven; but he that doeth the will of my Father which is in heaven. Many will say to me in that day, Lord, Lord, have we not prophesied in thy name? and in thy name have cast out devils? and in thy name done many wonderful works?

—Matthew 7:21–22

Could this warning be why the apostle Paul warned us to work out our salvation with fear and trembling?

In an earlier portion of the Sermon on the Mount, Christ warns us when we pray not to "babble like the heathen!" What did He mean? Idolatrous religions at the time of Christ used loud music and drums with mindless simple sing-song phrases repeated over and over, causing the worshippers to move and dance and increase their level of fanatical "worship" to the point of total loss of individual control. *Those who would introduce pagan music into the sanctuary ignore this warning.*

Wolves in Sheep's Clothing

All false religions demand at some point for the believer to abandon logic and self-control and surrender their mind to outside forces. Supposedly this heightens worship and makes it more emotional, more intense. It certainly does that, but it is false worship, demonically driven, and very dangerous. One of the things I personally discovered after years of pursuing the wrong gods in the wrong way through Christian Science, yoga, visualization, self-hypnosis, Scientology, astrology, and necromancy, was that at some point I was asked to surrender my mind and my being to forces outside of myself.

The only safe surrender is to Jesus Christ and He never, never, never asks us to abandon reason, logic, or personal intellectual and emotional control of our minds and bodies. In fact, one of the fastest ways of spotting a false religion is the eventual demand of all them to do this, in one way or another. *Don't do it!* This type of surrender is spiritual suicide and can only guarantee you a permanent reservation in Hell.

All false religions demand, at some point to stop thinking, to turn off your logical deductive reasoning. Why? Because from that point on, their faith shows their true colors, which are to help the demonic forces of evil invade your mind. In almost every instance the cults mentioned above used hypnotic, repetitive chanting, music, and/or dancing to help break down individual consciousness to the point that a demonic force can invade your mind.

True biblically-based Christianity never demands a surrender of your intellect or reasoning mind. In fact, God wants you to *maximize* your mind through the power of the Holy Spirit. Colossians 2 states that Jesus Christ is the source of all wisdom and knowledge. Whenever I do not know what to do or what to say, I claim this promise and ask the Lord for guidance. *This is all done consciously without surrender of my intellect.*

> Come now, and let us reason together, saith the LORD: though your sins be as scarlet, they shall be as white as snow; though they be red like crimson, they shall be as wool. If ye be *willing and obedient*, ye shall eat the good of the land: But if ye *refuse and rebel*, ye shall be devoured with the sword: for the mouth of the LORD hath spoken it.
>
> —Isaiah 1:18–20

Music of Rebellion

Rock music—Christian or non-Christian—is the music of rebellion. Samuel warned King Saul that God saw rebellion in the same light as he saw idolatry:

> And Samuel said, Hath the LORD as great delight in burnt offerings and sacrifices, as in obeying the voice of the LORD? Behold, *to obey is better than sacrifice, and to hearken than the fat of rams. For rebellion is as the sin of witchcraft, and stubbornness is as iniquity and idolatry.* . . .
>
> —1 Samuel 15:22–23

Those churches that hope to boost their attendance and membership by introducing pagan music into the sanctuary are in a state of rebellion. They have deliberately ignored scriptural warnings, two thousand years of tradition, the inner voice of the Holy Spirit, and just plain common sense. *Worldly music does not belong in worship.* Changing the words means nothing; in fact, it is an even greater sin before holy and righteous God, for you have connected the sacred with the profane, an unequally-yoked union that will not produce good fruit.

The only thing to which champions of Christian rock music can point to defend themselves is church growth—"Look at our membership!" Has the church historically ever been caught up large numbers? Yes, Jesus died for every sinner on this planet on the cross on Calvary, but Christ Himself said that few would find the path to salvation; and even those that did, as the parable of the sower in Matthew 13 illustrates, will hang onto their salvation and produce good fruit.

A Challenge

The Holy Spirit, prayer, a commitment to scriptural accuracy and presentation, evangelism, and a strong commitment to missionary outreach and children's ministries are what build a healthy church. The early Christian church grew rapidly during times of great persecution because the early church relied on the Holy Spirit to guide and build their church. All nonscriptural teachings were disallowed and any music that was derived from common pagan worship practices was forbidden.

God has given me a unique point of view on rock music in the church. I have experienced the damaging effects of pagan religion and their hypnotic music. I have studied thoroughly the demon-driven tribal religions of Africa, India, Tibet, Indonesia, and Polynesia for my book *All That Jazz: A History of Afro-American Music* (available through *amazon.com*).

I have learned how to manipulate people's emotions with music through my experiences in writing music for Hollywood films, television, and commercials. I have studied the growth of popular music in the twentieth century and was administrative director of Jazz Studies at the University of Southern California for many years. I am an experienced classical/pop/jazz musician, arranger, and composer, as well as a well-trained church musician with many years' experience in that field. I challenge any champion of rock music in the church to debate me—anytime, anywhere.

I truly believe that there can be no defense for the paganization of worship except for the ego-satisfaction of church growth and worldly rewards. I believe Christian rock musicians are in rebellion and need to repent, as well as those who have allowed the devil to slink into the sanctuary through the powerful force of music.

I urge all those who would challenge my point of view to not only study this book carefully, but also read my other books *Crisis in Christian Music*, *All That Jazz: A History of Afro-American Music*, and *The Power of Music*.

Another wonderful book out today is Dan Lucarini's *Why I Left the Contemporary Christian Music Movement* (Evangelical Press). His honest description of his growing disillusionment with rock music in the church and his courage to abandon his comfortable musical position and expose the spiritual deception of this music is a must read for anyone who honestly wants the truth.

What Is Truth?

Someone is right; someone is wrong. There can be no compromise in this arena. Your personal spiritual destiny is being affected by your position on this hot topic. Don't sweep it under the rug, and don't back away from challenging worship leaders, music leaders, pastors, elders, deacons, and even denominations, as well as the artist's themselves.

A Warning

Apostasy: A deliberate repudiation and abandonment of one's professed faith (Heb. 3:12). An aggressive and climactic revolt against God that will prepare the way for the appearance of the man of sin (2 Thess. 2:3).

Apostates are not true believers: There is a difference between someone who denies the faith out of fear and then returns to it, as the apostle Peter did, and someone who *categorically rejects it* (Deut. 13:13; 1 John 2:19).

Apostates will flourish in the last days (2 Thess. 2:3; 1 Tim. 4:1–3; 2 Tim 3:1–5).

Apostates will be punished (2 Pet. 2:17–22).

New evangelical Christian churches in Africa, Russia, and Eastern Europe, as well as the underground church in China, the Sudan, and South Korea *all reject contemporary Christian music* as being inappropriate and nonscriptural, unsuitable for worship and edification. Shouldn't that get our attention?

Salvation Army: Onward Christian Soldiers

Toward the end of the nineteenth century, a British general by the name of Booth became concerned about the growing number of homeless and helpless in London and other parts of Great Britain. A Christian, God gave him a vision in a dream one night to start an army, a Christian army that would invade the hell-holes of darkness in the major cities around the world and bring food, clothing, shelter, retraining, hope, and salvation to a countless number of sinners that the rest of society had ignored.

Music was an important part of their ministry.

The British "brass band" became their model and Salvation Army bands sprung up around the world. It's been over one hundred years now, and this solid Christian organization *has never once been tempted to use worldly music to attract converts.* God bless 'em and I wish more churches and church pastors, elders, music leaders, and members today would imitate their success in being obedient to God's Word.

Every year when they march in the world-famous *Rose Bowl Parade* from Pasadena, California, on New Year's Day, they march playing "Onward Christian Soldiers," not some warmed-over rock melody. God bless 'em again—I only wish more of us would take heed to their example.

Guidelines

Crisis in Christian Music, vol. 1, gives very specific guidelines for objectively determining music appropriate for worship. I refer the reader to that list. In addition and as part of a review I add the following:

Volume. There is no reason for worship music to be so loud that it makes the singer/listener uncomfortable. Rather than putting the person in a state of comfortable, relaxed worship, extreme volume creates tension, triggers the "fight-of-flight" response, and paganizes worship. Keep the volume down.

Instruments. I see no reason to bring amplified instruments into the church. The sounds they produce are inseparable in the listener's mind from commercial rock music. Drums are particularly dangerous because of their ability to trigger sensual responses as well as demonic rhythmic codes that can literally "call down" demons while worshiping.

I believe that supportive instruments in worship should be acoustic. If the sanctuary is large, there may be a need to mike softer acoustic instruments to be heard. Acoustic instruments amplified through a microphone and in-house PA system have a softer sound with a less harsh, trajectory-like signal cone when the sound is dispersed throughout the sanctuary.

So, no drums . . . ever. No electric guitar, electric bass, or electric synthesizer. These instruments are immediately associated with secular rock and detract from a true worshipful experience. If you must use some of these instruments, use guitar, synth, and bass. *Keep the drums out of the sanctuary. They do nothing but confuse the listener and introduce potentially dangerous rhythms, as well as suggesting a secular "sock hop" instead of a worship service.*

Lyrics. The lyrics of the songs selected should be clear, concise, and scripturally based. Monotonous songs with many repetitions of a single line *are dangerous.* This kind of repetition can induce the early stages of hypnosis and are contrary to historical worship practices of the Protestant Christian church. Compare the lyrics of some of the more simplistic contemporary "praise" songs with traditional hymns and spirituals from the past. There is no comparison. One sounds like a nursery rhyme; the other reflects spiritual maturity and meaning. *All lyrics should be easily understood—no rock 'n roll mumbling, no "Jesus is my buddy" over-personalized lyrics.*

Selection of Songs. The selection should be balanced between traditional hymns and spirituals and contemporary songs. The songs should balance each other in style and contrast. *Avoid performing traditional hymns and spirituals with a rock beat.* That is not only a distraction, it is an insult to older members of the congregation. *Utilize a cappella singing as often as possible* (unaccompanied). The early church sung everything a cappella. An elaborate accompaniment is not needed for every tune.

Dress. Musicians in a worship service are not performers or entertainers; they are priests assisting in a worship service. *They should be dressed uniformly, neatly, and certainly in contrast to rock musicians.* Again, the wrong message is sent to the congregation when the leaders of the praise and worship part of the service are dressed like the cover group of *Rolling Stone* magazine. Yes, and ladies, dresses, not jeans or slacks. Gentlemen, cut your hair, trim your beard and/or moustache. ZZ Top imitators are not appreciated. Dress is vitally important. Unity is emphasized when uniformity is part of the dress code, i.e., all white shirts, black pants or skirts, i.e., color coordinated.

Pep Talk

Your average Christian rock musician will rebel at these restrictions since presenting an aura of rebellious defiance is part of their persona. Explain to them this is not a rock arena, but a church. They are not just musicians, but priests assisting worship. Remind them that Christ said we should be servants. Humility is the number one virtue. Tell them to leave their worldly pride at the door.

Code of Ethics

All musicians must sign and agree to abide by a specific code of ethics:

1. They must be "saved" in the John 3 sense and openly acknowledge Jesus Christ as their Lord and Savior.
2. They cannot be users of drugs or alcohol or an active adulterer or fornicator. They cannot be a practicing homosexual. They are priests. Priests

have standards. Throughout the Bible, failure to live by God's standards when participating in leading worship is always punished severely.

3. They must agree to the dress code, to keeping the volume down, and to accepting the fact that some popular contemporary Christian songs are not necessarily appropriate for worship. After all, this is not Dick Clarke's "American Bandstand"; it is a gathering of believers to lift up their voices and hands in humble worship to their God and Creator and His Son, Jesus Christ.

4. There has to be a leader. Co-op groups may work in the rock world, but not in church. The group's leader should be both musically and spiritually mature and willing to submit to the authority of the pastor and the leaders of the church. The leader will make all final decisions on personnel, dress, repertoire, rehearsal schedules, etc. Input from the group's members will be welcome, but the final decision is in the hands of the leader. The leader can be male or female.

5. Body language while performing must be appropriate and seemly for worship. Sometimes praise groups who perform Saturday night in the local night club bring some of the same moves, winks, and show-biz magic into the sanctuary. Leave it at home. Movement on stage is okay, but should be appropriate to the music and worshipful in every instance. Remember that the eyes of the congregation are on you. Your body language and attitudes send a signal to them. Be careful what you send.

6. Applause will not be encouraged; in fact, it is recommended to remind the congregation that applause is not appropriate in worship service, unless it is for the King of Kings. Applause sets up an entertainment mode, with very few exceptions, and completely changes the worship service into a live performance.

7. The worship team should gather and pray together before the service. A few moments of silence during prayer should be observed so each person can *silently* confess any sins of omission (Oops, I forgot!) or commission (Darn! Why did I have to do that?) that happened during the week between services. Forgive any and everyone who has hurt you, and ask the Holy Spirit to fill you during the service. Pray for the unsaved. *Worship teams that do not sincerely pray before service always have problems of one kind or the other. They are priests who have gone into the sanctuary unclean;*

God will reject their worship.

8. No CDs, T-shirts, posters, etc. of the house music and worship team should be on display anywhere in the sanctuary (patio is okay). Announcements regarding concerts, etc., should be made at the very beginning of the service or printed in the bulletin.

9. Last-minute substitutes must make the rehearsal before the service. All subs must be confessed believers and participate in the before-service prayer with the worship team. It is better to perform without a sub than have a non-believer or someone who has not rehearsed with the ensemble. One way around this is to have "subs" rehearse regularly with the group but only perform when needed, or to have two separate praise ensembles that rehearse together but rotate services.

10. A good sign to put above the entrance to the rehearsal room is, *Leave your egos at the door.* That includes the choir director or praise band director. I've seen as many "prima donnas" in Christian music as I have seen in the secular music world, maybe more. My, oh my, it takes so little for Satan to puff us up! Just remember there is only one big shot in the Christian church, and that is Jesus Christ.

11. The eleventh commandment: *"Thou shalt not speak evil of thy fellow musician."* There is no place for ego or personality clashes in Christian music. If you can't keep your ego in check and remain a humble servant, then maybe you don't belong in music ministry. I have seen feuds between singers and musicians that went on for *years.*

12. It is the music director's responsibility to stop these things before they get out of hand. Remember the devil is *always* trying to divide the body of Christ. He will work overtime to bring division to the worship leaders if he can. Don't let him. Remember two sentences; use them often: *"I'm sorry"* and *"That's okay; I forgive you."* Don't wait until you feel like saying these things; in fact, they work best when you *least* feel like saying them

Please remember that it is an honor to lead worship of the King of Kings. Christ gave you the talent and the desire. Use it, knowing that He selected you for this role before you were born. Be humble, be grateful, and be full of love and joy. You have the privilege of leading worship of the King of Kings!

Stand Up!

It's time to take a stand in your church. If contemporary Christian rock has invaded your church, stand up to the challenge! This book and my previous book, *Crisis in Christian Music*, should give you enough ammunition to argue objectively against this worldly attempt to pollute the sanctuary and paganize worship.

Do not be intimidated by those who would accuse you of "dividing the brethren"! Christ expects us to stand up! Not once, but twice He drove the moneychangers from the Temple. He said that they did not belong in "his Father's house." Would Jesus do any less today?

Ask for a meeting with your pastor. Explain your feelings regarding contemporary Christian rock music and its unsuitability for worship. Give him copies of my books. Argue humbly and with love and respect from a (1) scriptural, (2) spiritual, (3) historical, and (4) physiological viewpoint of the dangers involved in letting this kind of secular music into the sanctuary for worship. Urge him to call, write, or e-mail me.

Arrange for a debate between someone who is solid in their reasons for opposing Christian rock music and someone who champions it. Let the chips fall where they may!

Bibliography

Books

Aiello, Rita and John Sloboada, *Musical Perceptions* (Oxford, UK: Oxford University Press, 1994)

Aitkin, Lindsay, *The Auditory Cortex: Structural and Functional Bases of Auditory Perception* (London: Chapman and Hall, 1990)

All God's Children and Blue Suede Shoes: Christians and Popular Culture (Westchester, IL: Crossways Books, 1989)

Baker, Paul, *Why Should the Devil Have All the Good Music?* (Waco, TX: Word Books, 1979)

Backus, John, *The Acoustical Foundations in Music* (New York: W. W. Norton, 1977)

Benson, Carl, ed., *The Bob Dylan Companion* (New York: Schirmer Books, 1998)

Berry, Wallace, *Structural Functions in Music* (Mineola, NY: Dover Publishing, 1987)

Booth, Stanley, *Keith* (New York: St. Martin's Press, 1995)

Broadbent, E. H., *Pilgrim Church* (Grand Rapids: Gospel Folio Press, 1999)

Broughton, Mark Ellingham, David Muddymand, and Richard Trillo, *The Rough Guide to World Music* (London: Penguin Books, 1994)

Campbell, Don, *The Mozart Effect* (New York: William Morrow & Co., 1997)

Colson, Chuck, *The Body* (Waco, TX: Word Books, 1992)

Edwards, Jonathan, *Sinners in the Hands of an Angry God* (New Kensington, PA: Whitaker House, 1997)

Green, Melody and David Hazard, *No Compromise* (Nashville: Sparrow Press, 1989)

Graham, Billy, *Just As I Am* (New York: HarperCollins, 1997)

Hanegraaff, Hank, *Counterfeit Revival* (Waco, TX: Word Books, 1997)

Hart, Mickey, *Drumming at the Edge of Magic* (Petaluma, CA: Grateful Dead Books, 1998)

Hayford, Jack W., *Worship His Majesty* (Waco, TX: Word Books, 1987)

Howard, David, *Acoustics and Psychoneurostics* (New York: Focal Press, 1990)

Joseph, Mark, *Rock and Roll Rebellion* (Nashville: Broadman & Holman, 1999)

Jourdan, Robert, *Music, the Brain, and Ecstasy* (New York: William Morrow & Co., 1997)

Lane, Deforia, *Music as Medicine* (Grand Rapids: Zondervan, 1994)

Learning to Worship as a Way of Life (Minneapolis: Bethany House, 1984)

Liesch, Barry, *The New Worship* (Grand Rapids: Baker Books, 1996)

Lewis, C. S., *The Business of Heaven* (New York: Harvest/HBJ, 1984)

Lucarini, Dan, *Why I Left the Contemporary Christian Movement* (CITY: Evangelical Press, 2002)

Medved, Michael, *Hollywood vs. America* (New York: Harper/Collins, 1992)

Meyer, Leonard, *Emotion and Meaning in Music* (NEED BIBLIO)

Miles, Elizabeth, *Tune Your Brain Using Music to Manage Your Mind, Body, and Moods* (CITY: Berkeley Publishing Group, 1998)

Morgenthaler, Sally, *Worship Evangelism* (Grand Rapids: Zondervan, 1995)

Music Physician: For Times to Come, Anthology (CITY: Quest Books, 1991)

Music Through the Eyes of Faith (San Francisco: Harper, 1993)

New Open Bible: New King James Translation (Nashville: Thomas Nelson, 1990)

Noebel, David, *Hypnotism and the Beatles: The Legacy of John Lennon*

----- *Rhythm, Riots, and Revolution* (BIBLIO)

Osbeck, Kenneth W., ed., *101 Hymn Stories* (Grand Rapids: Kregel Publishing, 1982)

----- *101 More Stories* (Grand Rapids: Kregel Publishing, 198)

Otis, George, *The Twilight Labyrinth* (CITY: Chosen Books, 1997)

Pass, David D., *Music and the Church: A Theology of Church Music* (Nashville: Broadman & Holman, 1989)

Peacock, Charlie, *At the Cross Roads (An Insider's Look at the Past, Present and Future of Contemporary Christian Music)* (Nashville: Broadman & Holman, 1999)

Religious Responses to Media and Pop Culture (CITY: PUBLISHER, 1998)

Robinson, Jennifer, *Music and Meaning* (CITY: Cornell University Press, 1997)

Rolling Stone Album Guide (New York: Random House, 1992)

Rossing, Thomas, *The Science of Sound* (CITY: Addison-Wesley Publishing, 1990)

Smith, Kimberly, *Let Those Who Have Ears to Hear* (CITY: PUBLISHER, 2001)

Starr, Anthony, *Music and the Mind* (CITY: Balantine Books, 1993)

The Hole in Our Soul: The Loss of Beauty and Meaning in American Popular Music (New York: The Free Press, 1994)

Tozer, A. W., *Whatever Happened to Worship?*, ed., Gerald B. Smith (Camp Hill, PA: Christian Publishing, 1985)

----- *Worship and Entertainment*, compiled by James Snyder (CITY: PUBLISHER, 1997)

Turner, Steve, *Hungry for Heaven* (Downer's Grove, IL: Intervarsity Press, 1995)

Warren, Rick, *The Purpose Driven Church* (Grand Rapids: Zondervan, 1993, rev. 1999).

Webster's Collegiate Dictionary, 2nd ed., (CITY: Simon & Schuster, 1978)

Wells, David F., *God in the Wasteland* (Grand Rapids: William B. Eerdmans, 1994)

Wheaton, Dr. Jack, *All That Jazz: A History of Afro-American Music* (NEED CITY: Scarecrow Press, NEED YEAR)

----- *Rock and Revolution* (San Diego: JCW Productions Inc., 1980)

----- *Technological and Sociological Influences on Jazz as an Art-Form in America* (CITY: University of Michigan Press, 1976)

Wilkerson, David, *Set the Trumpet to Thy Mouth* (CITY: PUBLISHER, 2000)

Articles

Andrews, John C., "Music in the Early Christian Church," *New Grove Dictionary of Music and Musicians,* ed., Stanley Sadie, 1980, Vol. 4, pp. 363–364

Barrier, Julie, "Contemporary Worship Trends," *International Resource Book for Church and School Musicians* (Nashville: Church St. Press), December 2000

Begley, Sharon, "Your Child's Brain," *Newsweek,* February 19, 1996

"Biology of Music, The" *The Economist,* London, England

"Brain Anatomy and Music," *Musica Research Notes,* Vol. VI, Issue 2, Spring 1999

Brewer, Jame F., "Healing Sounds," *Complementary Therapies in Nursing and Midwifery,* an international journal, Vol. 4, No. 1, April 24, 1998

Camp, Steve, "A Call for Reformation in the Contemporary Christian Music Industry," a poster/essay accompanied by 107 theses made public, October 31, 1997

"Making Music Makes You Smarter," NAMM, 5790 Armada Dr., Carlsbad, CA 92008; e-mail: *namm@namm.com*

Manning, Jacquiline, RGN, "Music Therapy," *British Journal of Theater Nursing,* Vol. 7. No. 3, June 1997

"Mozart Effect, The: A Small Part of the Big Picture," *Musica Research Notes,* Vol. VII, Issue 1, Winter 2000

Petrie, Phil, "The History of Gospel Music," *CCM Magazine,* February 1996

Rabey, Steve, "A Noebel Cause: The Constant Crusader Shares His Rhetoric on Rock," *CCM Magazine,* May 1986, pp. 23–25

----- "Silver Anniversary: Marantha!", *CCM Magazine,* November 1996

Rykov, Mary, MA, MTA; Deborah Salmon, MA, MTA, CMT, "Bibliography for Music Therapy ('63–'97)," *The American Journal of Hospice and Palliative Care,* Vol. 15, No. 3, May/June 1998

"Scientific Studies Have Proven That Music Participation Enhances Vital Intellectual Skills in Children," NAMM, Iowa Alliance for Arts Education

Weiss, Joanna, "The So-Called Mozart Effect May Be Just a Dream," *Boston Globe,* ISSUE DATE

Weiss, Rick, "Music Therapy," American Music Therapy Association, Silver Springs, MD

Westley, Marian, "Music Is Good Medicine," *Newsweek,* September 21, 1998, pp. 103–104

Wheaton, Jack, "Do's and Don'ts in Hiring Pros for Church Programs," *International Resource Book for Church and School Musicians* (Nashville: Church St. Press), December 2000

Magazines, Periodicals

American Music Therapy Association Inc., 8455 Colesville Rd. #1000, Silver Springs, MD 20910

Contemporary Christian Music, ADDRESS, Nashville, Tenn.

Worship Leader Magazine, 107 Kenner Ave., Nashville, TN 37205

CDs, Audio Tapes

Acoustic Hymns (classical guitar, keyboards, and small choral group —25 favorites)

At the Foot of the Cross—selected artists: Amy Grant, Sandi Patti, Brian Duncan, etc.

Cathedrals Anthology: Favorite Gospel Quartet—35 years of music

Contemporary Christian Music in the Church and in the Home, Focus on the Family, 1984

Counterfeit Revival: Looking for God in all the Wrong Places, Hank Hanigraff (Waco: Word Audio)

Favorite Christmas Carols, Vol. 1, Dr. Jack Wheaton (Oklahoma City: Hearthstone Publishing, 1999)

Favorite Hymns, Vol. 1, Dr. Jack Wheaton (Oklahoma City: Hearthstone Publishing, 2000)

Found A Place (FFH) acoustic pop sound

He Touched Me: The Gospel Music of Elvis Presley (2-CD set)

Hymns of Our Faith (4-CD collection), Christian Book Distributors

If That Isn't Love, George Beverly Shea

Maranatha: 25th Anniversary

Millennium Worship—Ron Kenoly, Alvin Slaughter, etc.

Strategic Trends Year 2000, Chuck Missler, (Coeur d'Alene, ID: Koinonia House)

The Best of Andrae Crouch

The Best of Bill Gaither and the Bill Gaither Trio

The Best of Carman

The Best of Sandi Patti

The Church's Music—H. B. London, Jr. (Focus on the Family)

The Classics—Ray Boltz

The Walk—Steven Curtis Chapman

Wow: Worship Collection (Integrity, Maranatha & Vineyard Music

Video Tapes, DVDs

Brooklyn Tabernacle Choir

Prince of Egypt, Steven Spielberg, Producer, 1998, 99 min.

The New Messiah (Concert Tour)

Wow 2000, The Videos (best music from your favorite artists)

About the Author

Dr. Wheaton, previous president of the *American Federation of Musicians*, San Diego Chapter, is currently directing the *Rancho Santa Fe Jazz Orchestra*, and leading the *San Diego Jazz Quartet*, and is also working on a new book, *The Power of Music*. He is also the official representative to colleges, universities, churches and private organizations for Steinway Pianos (NW). He has taught a course on the history of jazz for the University of California San Diego, using his best-selling text, *All That Jazz*, (Scarecrow Press and available through *amazon,com*) and has many lecture-series at the Atheneum in LaJolla, California, the most recent being on *The Blues*. Jack Wheaton has an earned doctorate in music, history, and education.

Dr. Wheaton is one of the original founders and *past president* of the *International Association of Jazz Educators*, and recently presented a research paper on *West Coast Jazz* at their convention in New York City in January 2004.

He is active as an administrator, performing musician (piano), composer/arranger/conductor, and nationally known historian, musicologist, author, lecturer, and adjudicator.

Prior to moving to San Diego, Dr. Wheaton was *administrative director of Jazz Studies* at the *University of Southern California, Los Angeles*. While in Los Angeles he was active as a film composer, writing the original musical scores for *Guns and the Fury* (MGM), *Cat in the Cage* (MGM), *Penitentiary II* (Warner Bros.), and other films.

The Stan Kenton Neophonic Orchestra premiered Dr. Wheaton's original composition *Phrygia* at the Dorothy Chandler Pavilion in Los Angeles in 1968.

That same year he became the conductor of the *Collegiate Neophonic Orchestra*, recorded a double LP for *Capitol Records*, and won an *Emmy Award* for conducting and original music for the ABC-TV Special, "Neophonic Spring."

He auditioned and helped train the 84 pianists for the "Rhapsody in Blue" opening ceremony segment of the 1984 Olympics in Los Angeles. He has conducted at the *Hollywood Bowl*, the *Rome Opera*, the *Kennedy Center*, and the *San Diego Civic Center*. He also trained the 88 pianists for the halftime show of the '88 Superbowl. Jack is the author of 14 books and has recorded 15 CDs. His Capitol Records recording of the Collegiate Neophonic has just been re-released through Tarantara Records. He can be reached at:

PO. Box 1331
Rancho Santa Fe, CA 92067
e-mail: *jcwprod@cox.net*
(858) 756-3190